Our Summer in the Vale of Kashmir

Our Summer In the Vale of Kashmir

F. Ward Denys

GOVERNMENT REPRINTS PRESS
Washington, D.C.

© Ross & Perry, Inc. 2001 All rights reserved.

No claim to U.S. government work contained throughout this book.

Protected under the Berne Convention. Published 2001

Printed in The United States of America
Ross & Perry, Inc. Publishers
717 Second St., N.E., Suite 200
Washington, D.C. 20002
Telephone (202) 675-8300
Facsimile (202) 675-8400
info@RossPerry.com

SAN 253-8555

Government Reprints Press Edition 2001

Government Reprints Press is an Imprint of Ross & Perry, Inc.

Library of Congress Control Number: 2001093055

http://www.GPOreprints.com

ISBN 1-931641-52-8

☉ The paper used in this publication meets the requirements for permanence established by the American National Standard for Information Sciences "Permanence of Paper for Printed Library Materials" (ANSI Z39.48-1984).

All rights reserved. No copyrighted part of this publication may be reproduced, stored in a retrieval system, or transmitted, in any form or by any means, electronic, photocopying, recording, or otherwise, without the prior written permission of the publisher.

DEDICATION

To all lovers of the beautiful this book is dedicated. For in the remote and fascinating Vale of Kashmir there is such a wealth of varied beauty that every taste can find a feast. When other lands have all been gleaned and memory is richly filled with precious treasures of countless scenes and lovely forms, an unrealized charm is still in store for every soul that has responded to the beautiful in all these diverse realms, for here, here in Kashmir, the sense of satisfaction is to many quite complete. This lofty Valley with its marvelous beauty seems very near the vault of heaven, and all that is best in man revives till the soul is fired to "hitch its chariot to a star."

PREFACE

THE title of this volume is happily chosen, "Our Summer in the Vale of Kashmir." We are indebted to Dr. Denys for making this land of poetry and song, known chiefly through the enchanting verses of "Lalla Rookh," so real and vital to us. The chapters are not only charming in their delightful portrayal of life in the Valley, but are also valuable for the painstaking presentation of details—the how and when and where of things that go to make up real living in a place. For this reason the book will doubtless prove to be of considerable assistance to tourists, and to those who may not yet have been so fortunate as to visit the Vale of Kashmir it will bring anticipations of enjoyment, and a longing desire to partake of the various phases of life to be experienced there in their fullness of beauty and interest.

The well-chosen pictures and the artistic letter-press will also add to the reader's pleasure and satisfaction.

Owing to this intimate touch gained through his long sojourn in the places he so picturesquely describes, Dr. Denys has produced a volume that is an important addition to works in lighter vein on countries too seldom visited. As the first American who has written of his experiences in the land of Kashmir, he will doubtless incite others of his countrymen to make the long journey and share with him in the varied charms of a region so aptly characterized by Dr. Arthur Neve:

"The Valley of Kashmir owes its fame, doubtless, not less to the wild grandeur of the barriers which surround it than to its own intrinsic loveliness. It is this contrast which has led the poets of all nations to speak of it as an 'emerald set in pearls.' But the varied beauties of Kashmir appeal to every

PREFACE

want and taste. For the cultivator of the soil, there is fertility of land, abundance of water, variety and plenty of natural products, whether grain or fruits. For the herdsman, there is rich pasturage and broad meadows. The sportsman finds game in the jungles and along the mountain-sides. The fisherman finds ample use for the rod, the artist for his sketch-block and colours, the archaeologist, linguist, botanist, or geologist, may well whet their enthusiasm over the stately Buddhist ruins, the luxuriant vegetation, or the many geological problems awaiting their investigations; while they who have neither hobbies nor inclinations, who want but rest and amusement in a lovely country and pleasant climate, can take their fill of Nature's bounty."

MITCHELL CARROLL.

CONTENTS

	PAGE
THE VALE OF KASHMIR	*Prologue*

I
WHERE IS KASHMIR?	29

II
HOTEL, HOUSEBOAT OR COTTAGE	38

III
THE DIANA	45

IV
THE SERVANTS	49

V
FOODS	56

VI
FINDING A PLACE	63

VII
THE PICTURESQUE RIVER	67

VIII
THE DHAL LAKE	76

IX
SHOPS AND BAZAARS	85

X
WOOD-CARVING AND SILVERWARE	93

XI
NATIVE INDUSTRIES	100

XII
SOCIAL LIFE	107

CONTENTS

		PAGE
XIII	THE RESIDENCY	115
XIV	THE MAHARAJA	123
XV	THE CLUB	134
XVI	SPORTS	141
XVII	VALLEY AND MOUNTAINS	148
XVIII	PLACES OF WORSHIP	152
XIX	ANCIENT TEMPLES	156
XX	HOSPITALS	167
XXI	SCHOOLS	177
XXII	HOUSEBOAT TRAVELING	185
XXIII	GANDERBAL	197
XXIV	ISLAMABAD	205
XXV	GULMARG	212
XXVI	THE PEOPLE	218
XXVII	AN ARTIST PARADISE	231

LIST OF ILLUSTRATIONS

	PAGE
Lotus Flowers of Dhal Lake	*Frontispiece*
In Colors from a Photograph	
The Temple that Crowns the Takht-i-Sulieman	16
Warmth of Color, Pearly Mist and Snow-Capped Mountains	22
Painted especially for this volume by Col. H. H. Hart, R. E.	
Bullock Carts on the Pass	28
Ekkas	28
The Rest-House of Domel	31
The Rest-House of Chakoti	31
The Outer Circular Road	36
In Colors from a Photograph	
At Baramulla	39
The Houseboat "Diana"	44
A Domestic Rice Mill	48
Primitive Suspension Bridge	53
A Food Bazaar	57
A Campers' Paradise	62
A Water Highway of Kashmir	66
In Colors from a Photograph	
The Winding Jhelum	69
On Kashmiri Waters	69
Beating Out the Rice	73
Nishat Bagh on Dhal Lake	77
One of the Seven Bridges	84
A Candy Kitchen of Kashmir	87
Two Panels of a Carved Screen	92
Examples of Wood-Carving	95
Wood-Carving and Engraving on Silver	97
Children Weaving Rugs	101
Papier Mâché, Silver, Brass and Wood	105
A Garden Party at the Residency	109
"We linger in beauties that never are gone"	114
Painted especially for this volume by Col. H. H. Hart, R. E.	
The Seventh Bridge	117
The British Residency	117

LIST OF ILLUSTRATIONS

	PAGE
A Living Welcome to the Maharaja	122
Prince Hari Singh	125
The Maharaja's Palace at Srinagar	129
Towing	129
The Maharaja and Cricket Teams	131
The Srinagar Club	135
The Entrance to Gulmarg	135
British Polo Team	140
Young Kashmir at Play	143
A Lowland Eight Thousand Feet Above the Sea	149
The English Church and Rectory	153
Pilgrims to the Cave of Amarnath	153
The Smaller Temple at Avantipur	157
The Ruined Temple of Bhaniyar	157
The Ancient Temple Ruins at Patan	162

In Colors from a Photograph

	PAGE
The Temple of Martund	165
The Temple of Pandrathan	165
Dr. Arthur Neve and Assistants	169
An Out-Ward of the Mission Hospital	169
A Native Hut in Atchibal	173
Welcoming His Highness	179
Killing the Demons of Wular Lake	184
From Srinagar to Baramulla	187
Nightfall on Wular Lake	192

Painted especially for this volume by Col. H. H. Hart, R. E.

	PAGE
Lidar Valley above Phalgram	196
The Lidar River at Gulmarg	196
Shisha Nag Glacier	199
Plowing in the Valley	204
Holy Men	209
The Royal Post Tonga	213
The Kashmir Sedan	213
Women Spinning Thread	219
Spinning Out the Thread	223
Traveling Musicians with Nautch Girls	225
Another Glimpse of Chenar Bagh	230
An Artist Paradise	233

Painted especially for this volume by Col. H. H. Hart, R. E.

THE ANCIENT TEMPLE THAT CROWNS THE TAKHT-I-SULIEMAN

For untold centuries the Faithful from the Valley far below have found their way to the top of the Takht, there to worship at this altar in the clouds. This ancient temple is rich in romantic history and the beacon tower for all of the Vale of Kashmir.

THE VALE OF KASHMIR

WITH all that has been said and sung of the Vale of Kashmir, its very name brings to the mind visions of a far-away land of transcendent beauty and charm, a kingdom of romance. To some, it is a name to conjure with and there are many under the spell of its call who turn their burning eyes away from the modern glare,

"the fretful stir
Unprofitable, and the fever of the world"

to gaze longingly toward this enchanting realm where time is not, where months are reckoned only by the flowers or fruit they bring—and believe that if once they might enter the Vale of Kashmir, there they would find their lost youth and lost dreams.

The dying Mogul Emperor Jehangir, when asked if he desired anything, closed his eyes as if to dream of the fair land he loved, as he made answer, "Only Kashmir."

Possessing every variety of climate and scenery and an equally varied past, Kashmir has never failed to satisfy the visitor who has been willing to undertake the long and arduous journey, whether in the old days when the Delhi Emperors traversed the difficult route on horseback and in palanquins with their splendid retinue, or as now, when the modern tourist reaches the promised land by passing from the hot and dusty railway train to the unreliable motor-car or jolting tonga.

With our fixed ideas of Kashmir as an Elysium where Nature has poured out lavishly her choicest gifts, where beauty vies with romance to weave a mystic spell, it is easy to credit the tales that when the earth was young, the Valley was under the special protection of the gods and that its soil nurtured demi-gods and heroes.

In prehistoric times, according to an old Sanskrit poet, a vast lake once covered the Valley. It was under the care of the goddess Pervati who was so friendly that when she sailed her boat over the lake, its waters became smooth and safe.

THE VALE OF KASHMIR

But a wicked dragon disputed her beneficent power. From the deep waters where he dwelt he caused storms to arise and overwhelm any boatmen who might venture to cross. Thus good and evil strove for the victory, but the dragon remained unconquered. Then the god Brahma sent his grandson to overcome the demon, but in vain. Whereupon the deities took counsel and struck the mountain a mighty blow, making a great cleft through which the waters of the lake rushed forth. Still the demon eluded them, cowering beneath the remaining water. At last the goddess Pervati came forth from her rocky height and in despair and anger hurled a mountain down upon the dragon in his hiding place, burying him under the mass of rock. The people will tell you today that this mountain imbedded in the ancient lake can still be seen, for it is the hill on which the fort Hari Parbat stands, built by Akbar, the great Mogul Emperor. At Baramulla, the present gorge and narrow channel testify to the cleft made in the mountain.

The fertile Valley invited men to dwell there, and it became populated by a primitive non-Aryan people who lived in the fear of demons and imagined the serpent a god. From these superstitions grew Nàg worship, the most ancient cult in Kashmir, which has left its mark in many names of places, as Nàg Marg, "the alp of the snake," and Vernàg, "the place of many springs and the snake." Their veneration for the snake led them to build tanks for the god to occupy at the springs, which became shrines and were regarded as sacred places.

The Aryan invaders found these primitive people in the Valley and in contrast to their well-demons and malignant spirits which must ever be placated, brought friendly and shining divinities with whom they stood on good terms. The old Aryan word *deva*, the shining one, has derivatives in religious use today.

Thus through the years arose the kingdom of Kashmir. But however favored by nature, its rich heritage brought misery upon the country and people, for it became the prey of envious neighbors and invading hordes. For over 2,000 years, with the exception of a few peaceful periods, it was racked and oppressed by alien rule. It passed from the grasp of Buddhists to Hindus, Mohammedans, Sikhs and again to Hindus before reaching the present era of an established government and general toleration.

THE VALE OF KASHMIR

When Alexander the Great, King of Macedon, entered northern India in 327 B. C. and pitched his camp on the river which he called Hydaspes, influences were started which were to bear upon the subsequent history of Kashmir for generations. The *fabulosus Hydaspes* of classic fame is the modern Jhelum, the great placid waterway of Kashmir. Not far from the southern boundary of Kashmir, where the river makes a bend, Alexander fought a battle in the course of which his beloved charger, the renowned Bucephalus, was slain. In his honor Alexander built a memorial city on the west bank of the river near the modern Jalalpur.

In Alexander's camp in the Punjab was an Indian adventurer, Chandra Gupta, who afterward seized a kingdom for himself, compelled Seleucus, Alexander's successor in India, who was ruling over Syria, to make a treaty with him and married the daughter of Seleucus, a Greek princess. It was Asoka, the grandson of this Indian king, who in 257 B. C. came to rule over Kashmir and who in 256 B. C. made a treaty with Antiochus II, the grandson of Seleucus. The Greeks had founded an independent Kingdom in Bactria, northwest of the Himalayas, and their territory extended nearly to the borders of Kashmir.

Along the Jhelum River in the Valley of Kashmir there are ancient temples which remind one more of Greece than of India. Naturally the theory presents itself that the Kashmiri architects must have borrowed their fluted columns, their porches and pediments from the temples of their Greek neighbors in Bactria. Dr. Arthur Neve says of the little temple of Pandrathan—"Its ceiling is the most purely classical design of any in Kashmir and might well pass for Greek work."

These ruined temples and shrines tell the story of Kashmir, but of them all, the interesting temple of Pandrathan, just mentioned, is most closely identified with the ancient and mediaeval history of the Valley, and it is the only one which has escaped the violence of invaders. The tank in which it stands dates back probably to the dim past when the primitive Nàg worship held sway. It remains the sole relic of the former splendid capital, the first Srinagar which flourished in the Hindu period before the seat of government was moved to the present capital, Srinagar,—the old Srinagar that knew the great king Asoka, who has been compared to Constantine, because he made Buddhism a state religion, Constantine

THE VALE OF KASHMIR

afterward effecting the same thing for Christianity. This old city must have been filled with rejoicing over the victories of the good native King Laladitya, whose beneficent reign was one of the few bright spots in all the centuries of oppression.

If the little temple did not see the old capital in its more prosperous days, it is the only remaining link with that past. When the city was destroyed by fire, the temple still stood unharmed. When five centuries later Sikander, the "idol breaker," was king, this was the only shrine to escape his violent hands. It saw the Hindu kingdom fall and witnessed five hundred years of Mohammedan rule, and beheld, in 1819, the victorious Runjit Singh occupy the Valley. It still bears witness to the nature-loving Moguls for some Mogul prince planted willows and plane trees to keep their kindly watch over the lonely temple bearing its burden of a thousand years.

The reign of Akbar the Great, the real founder of the Mogul Empire, was contemporary with that of Queen Elizabeth of England. He conquered Kashmir in 1587 and quelled its last revolt in 1592. It was he who built the fort Hari Parbat on the mountain which the goddess Pervati, according to the legend, threw down upon the dragon. He thus gave employment to thousands and instituted various public works. Not only great wealth came into the Valley with the magnificence of the Delhi Court, but other advantages and it is to Akbar, it is said, that Srinagar owes the Garden of the Morning Wind, the Nasim Bagh, on the shores of the Dhal Lake. Prince Selim was Akbar's favorite son, and, according to the annals, he was the one who was always sent to quell any revolt or trouble in the empire. He succeeded his father and became the Emperor Jehangir. Romance in the history of Kashmir centres in the reign of this Emperor and his beloved queen, Nur Mahal. As Empress she came to be the principal figure in the Mogul Court and was known as Nur Jahan, "the light of the world."

Born in dire poverty, though of a noble Persian family, her beauty won the heart of the young prince and their love endured through many vicissitudes until they were at last united. Their devotion continued through life and they were never happier than when, throwing aside the cares and trappings of state, they wandered through their lovely gardens in the Vale of Kashmir. It was the Emperor's pleasure to indulge his beautiful wife in her plans for these royal gardens, which with

THE VALE OF KASHMIR

their marble terraces and stately walks, fountains and waterfalls, noble trees and fragrant blossoms were to add to the happiness of unborn generations. What matter if the marble had to be brought from far off Delhi and the skilled workmen, too? It was joy enough to linger beside the fountain while Nur Mahal played with the shining fishes, or to rest in the shade of the plane trees, or beneath the marble portals while soft music mingled with the song of the waterfall.

It was this Emperor's son, Shah Jehan, who built at Agra the exquisite mausoleum of Taj Mahal, a dream frozen in marble. He erected it in memory of his wife, Arjamand Benu, who died in 1631.

Under Shah Jehan, the Mogul Empire reached its greatest strength and magnificence. Shah Jehan's land revenues amounted to more than $120,000,000, including Kashmir and five provinces in Afghanistan. With the death of his son, the last great Mogul Emperor, Aurangzeb, in 1707, the people became, in the words of Sir Alfred Lyall, "a masterless multitude prepared to acquiesce in the assumption of authority by anyone who could show himself able to discharge the most elementary functions of government in the preservation of life and property."

It has been said that the establishment of British dominion in India has no parallel in the history of the world. For while other empires have been established by series of conquests carried out overland, England's power in India has been won by the sea, and from the years of maritime exploration and small coast settlements, its growth has been development brought about by inevitable forces.

The Valley of Kashmir at the close of the Sikh wars was recognized by the British as an independent state under their protection. It was brought into closer relations with India by the establishment of a British resident at the capital, Srinagar, after the accession of the new Maharaja in 1885.

Jammu is a feudatory state of the Maharaja of Kashmir, who comes from a Dogra-Rajput family. This signifies that he is of famous military stock. The word Rajput means "sons of princes." Its use goes back to the time when the Aryan Hindu invaders came down from the north into India and separated into three divisions—the soldiers, the Brahmans, or priests, and the general civil population. Through all the years the soldier class has made a great record in military history.

THE VALE OF KASHMIR

The Maharaja's Dogra ancestors belonged also to the old Aryan Hindu race and were noted for their courage and great physical endurance. His force of Imperial Service troops consists mainly of Dogras and at the outbreak of the present war, the Maharaja placed them immediately at the disposal of the British Government. In addition, he subscribed a large sum to the Fund of His Royal Highness, the Prince of Wales, and also gave generously to the Indian Fund. Not content with that, he did something rather unusual for an Indian prince. The Marquess of Crewe, Secretary of State for India, is the authority for an account of how "the Maharaja of Kashmir presided at a meeting of two thousand people in Srinagar and himself delivered a stirring speech, as the result of which large subscriptions were collected."

It is impossible to give here any idea of the great work for India under the British Government, which is going on with increasing results. In the words of Nawab Nizamut Jung, High Court Judge of Hyderabad:

> "Unmindful of their ancient name
> And lost to Honour, Glory, Fame,
> And sunk in strife,
> Thou found'st them, whom thy touch has made
> Men, and to whom thy breath conveyed
>   A nobler life!"

OUR SUMMER IN THE
VALE OF KASHMIR

Bullock carts on the pass. These unique freight trains of Kashmir are allowed to travel only at night, so that the road may be free for other travel during the day.

Transportation, the world-old problem of man, has been solved in Kashmir by means that make for sureness rather than speed. These odd two-wheeled ekkas are used mostly to bring tourists into the Valley.

I

WHERE IS KASHMIR?

> "Who has not heard of the Vale of Cashmere,
> With its roses the brightest that earth ever gave,
> Its temples, and grottos, and fountains as clear
> As the love-lighted eyes that hung over their wave?"
> —*Lalla Rookh.*

TO some this may seem an entirely unnecessary question, and the only excuse I have for considering it is that before I met friends who had lived there my own notions of it were extremely vague and intangible, and such as I had were associated for the most part with "Lalla Rookh" and its exuberant rhetoric and poetic license. This was due I presume to shadowy memories of the days when I was a student of English literature. I knew, of course, that there was such a spot as Kashmir, and it is barely possible that I may have been asked to give its boundaries when I was studying geography, but until I had looked it up on the map and read all I could find about it, my notions of it were very nebulous. Moreover, even after I had read all that I could find upon the subject and learned from friends who had lived in the Valley what they had to say about it, my conception of it was still rather indefinite.

It was, of course, easy to see that it was on the northern boundary of India, with Thibet to the east, Turkestan to the north, and Afghanistan to the west. One wag even made it a part of India. But it was not until I had actually reached Srinagar that I realized what its geographic and civic relation was to the Indian Empire. Guide-books say that it is a valley about twenty miles wide and eighty miles long, surrounded by lofty, snow-capped mountains, and that two striking elevations rise from its midst; that it has two large lakes, and that a winding river runs throughout its entire length. But no one had told me that, although the elevation of the Valley is above five thousand feet, the climate is not

THE VALE OF KASHMIR

as exhilarating as that of the Adirondacks, with an elevation of only fourteen hundred feet, or Eagles Mere, Pennsylvania, with an elevation of two thousand two hundred feet, or Oberhofen on Lake Thun at nineteen hundred feet. Still, anyone can see from the map that its principal city, Srinagar, is almost on the same parallel as that of Los Angeles and Yokohama, but south of the Riviera, northern Africa and Spain, and thus find an explanation for this lack of tonic quality in April, the time our visit began.

While all this may not make it very clear just where Kashmir is, a careful study of the map will help to identify this portion of the world which is little known and seldom visited by any but Englishmen; for rarely do Germans, Frenchmen, Italians, Spaniards, or in short any Europeans, go there. Nor for that matter do many American tourists stray so far from the beaten path as this. They have the reputation of going almost everywhere in great numbers and distributing dollars in large and liberal quantities all along the way, and while it may be true that some have done much to destroy many an economical paradise, because of these extravagant habits of spending money, it cannot justly be said that they are mean or niggardly simply because they now and then refuse to pay three or four times as much as would be charged Europeans, or because they decline to give tips that are two or three times as much as the natives expect from tourists from other countries.

But to return to the map—being careful to consult one that shows the railroads—you will see that there is no station nearer this Valley than Rawal Pindi, and that one of the rivers flows from the Valley down into northern India. It will also become evident that it is in the midst of a mountainous country, and that to reach it means a long voyage by steamer to India, and many miles of railroad travel before the entrance to the pass is gained.

As to the question, how to get to Kashmir, much naturally depends upon the part of the world the reader is in, though

The charmingly situated rest-house of Domel. Despite the grandeur of the scenery, the hospitable rest-houses nestled in the hills at frequent intervals form welcome breaks in the two hundred-mile journey into the Valley.

At this point the road is flanked by precipitous mountain walls, to whose sides cling immense boulders, which seem to offer a real menace to the wayfarer and the pleasant rest-house of Chakoti.

THE VALE OF KASHMIR

wherever he may be, it will, first of all, be necessary to go to some Indian port. Letters from New York take about a month, and from London about three weeks, to reach there. From San Francisco it takes longer still, and from most European cities less time than from London. It is, therefore, a matter of steamship journey from wherever you happen to be to any Indian port that may suit you best. It then becomes a question of a railroad journey to Rawal Pindi, that being the usual starting point from the railroad for travelers going to the Valley of Kashmir. And Rawal Pindi can be reached by rail from Tuticorin, Madras, Calcutta, Bombay or Karachi, with but few, if any, changes of cars. The last is, perhaps, the nearest port in actual distance, though passengers who have tried that way say the steamers to other ports are larger and better and the railroad journey more comfortable than from Karachi. We decided to go from Bombay, and were very much gratified to find that the cars were well-equipped and very comfortable—far more so than we had expected.

We took our train one evening and after traveling all that night we passed through Delhi about ten o'clock the following night, and then continued through Amritzar and Lahore to Rawal Pindi, where we arrived the day following in the afternoon. It was therefore a little less than two days' journey. But in spite of the excessive heat it was fairly comfortable, as all our meals were taken in the dining-car on the train, with the exception of one at Lahore. The compartments were each about nine feet long and the full width of the car, with a divan upholstered in leather on either side, running lengthwise of the car. They were all provided with commodious toilet- and dressing-rooms, and the better ones were not only lighted by electricity, but had two electric fans, one with a moistening attachment that had a very refreshing effect upon the air. The divans were used as beds at night, and a third one could be let down from the side above the windows if it was desired. There were also two large easy chairs in each of these compartments. We were told that some of the trains had cars with

THE VALE OF KASHMIR

large and well-appointed bathrooms, but as we were anxious to reach the Valley as soon as possible, we did not wait for one of these.

As all the station-masters speak English and many of the attendants understand it, even ladies sometimes travel without a bearer or native servant. We would, however, always strongly recommend taking one, for they are not only useful as interpreters, but render a great variety of practical services. For instance, they make up your beds, relieve you of all trouble about your luggage, and secure your cabs for you at the railroad station, as well as serve as guides in visiting places of interest.

From Rawal Pindi, which, as already stated, is the station where you leave the train, you can go into the Valley in one of several ways, either by motor-car, landau or tonga. The first usually takes two days, although it is less than two hundred miles to Srinagar, but the objection to the motor-car is that if it breaks down—an all-too-frequent occurrence—a very annoying delay may result. The landau is in some respects the most comfortable and certain mode of conveyance, at least many people think so, but it is much more expensive and only carries four passengers and but little or no luggage. The tonga, which is the usual mode of travel, is a covered conveyance on two wheels with seats for three in addition to the driver, and places for two small trunks above the wheels on either side, while above these bedding and traveling rugs are often tied on. It is drawn by one or two horses, according to the tariff paid by the passenger, and takes three, four, five or six days, according to the number of horses and the frequency of changes on the way. With either a landau or a tonga, and a sufficient number of changes of horses, the entire journey can be made quite comfortably with but two nights on the way, and as the rest-houses are for the most part very good indeed, and some are charmingly situated, this is often a very delightful experience. Some indeed find the ride so agreeable that they prefer to take the longer time of six

THE VALE OF KASHMIR

days, not only because the fares are less, but also on account of the greater ease of riding the shorter distances each day, and the agreeable novelty of putting up at some of these picturesque and charming rest-houses.

A very good way to make the journey is to stop for the first night at the beautiful hill station of Murree, where there are two hotels, and then take two nights between there and Baramulla. Here you can arrange to have your houseboat waiting for you and go on in this way up the river in your floating home to Srinagar at your leisure. Although, if you prefer to do so, you can continue in your traveling conveyance to this destination. These boats can be hired from agents in Rawal Pindi if they have not already been engaged by correspondence with Srinagar. You can also make arrangements in regard to them at Baramulla, though the selection is naturally much larger in Srinagar, where there is a very large number of boats affording a wide variety of choice.

II

HOTEL, HOUSEBOAT OR COTTAGE

> "Or to see it by moonlight—when mellowy shines
> The light o'er its palaces, gardens, and shrines".
> —*Lalla Rookh.*

AFTER arriving in Srinagar, if the question of quarters has not already been settled in advance through an agent or friend living there, it can readily be arranged according to your own wishes and tastes. The hotel is a good one with large airy rooms and balconies, and the table is also good for India, or as hotels average in India, and should you decide to stay in it, you will be free from all the annoyances of housekeeping—and there are plenty of them even in Kashmir—as well as escape, in some measure, the eternal—many say infernal—servant question. But you will lose to a large extent all the advantages of a home, with freedom to control the kind and quality of your food, as it is impossible for any hotel, however obliging, to consider all the individual tastes and whims of its patrons. Therefore, if you wish to be free to choose your own diet and the way you wish your food prepared and served, it becomes a question of a cottage or houseboat.

Of the former there are a few to be had, but as the best are taken by the year and are available only when the tenant is willing to sublet, the choice is not an extensive one. We learned of several such cottages, though, and some of them were delightfully situated and attractively furnished. If it suits you to take a cottage, the chances are it will have an attractive flower garden, a well-stocked fruit and vegetable garden, and a stable. It will therefore be merely a matter of getting servants and moving in, and this will only mean going to the hotel first and then looking about until you find a cottage that answers your purpose.

But by far the large majority live in houseboats, and some remain in them not only during the spring and autumn months,

AT BARAMULLA

Where the traveler gets his first glimpse of native life on the Jhelum. It is nothing short of marvelous how many people live in one of these small houseboats, as there is never less than one family and sometimes several. Also here at Baramulla is first encountered the native method of bridge construction.

THE VALE OF KASHMIR

but all summer, or in a few instances throughout the entire year. The latter admit that it is sometimes a little hot and the mosquitoes somewhat troublesome, but claim that they are not seriously uncomfortable at any time, and that there are always compensations for the stay-at-homes even on houseboats.

The selection of the houseboat by no means concludes one's living arrangements, unless by chance he has selected one that is a combination of houseboat and kitchen boat. It is necessary in most instances to engage a kitchen boat along with the houseboat. This is arranged in such a way that the front portion is devoted to a kitchen for the occupants of the houseboat. In this there are two or three stoves—not stoves after the fashion that we are accustomed to, but merely earthen or cement constructions with a hole in the top and in which a fire can be built. They are very simple and primitive, and yet on these stoves almost anything one is accustomed to have in a western home is prepared with great success. In this department also are the boxes for holding the food, that is, the meats and vegetables and articles of that description, and underneath the floor there is a large space for storing wood. In the rear of this is another compartment that may be subdivided by curtains and here are the quarters of the more important servants. In the rear of the boat there is a large section devoted to the boatmen and their wives and families. As this community is sometimes quite numerous, and is provided with their own stove and cooking arrangements, it is hard to understand how they are all able to live in such contracted quarters. It will be seen at once that by having the kitchen boat in the rear of the houseboat, little or no odor from the cooking ever reaches the occupants of the latter, and, curiously enough, although there were a large number of people always on this boat, we rarely, if ever, heard any sounds coming from it. For this kitchen boat, including the services of three men, with their wives and families, one pays the large sum of five dollars a month.

THE VALE OF KASHMIR

There are also one or two rowboats to be hired in connection with the houseboat. These have their paddles and awnings and cushions, and as a rule are very comfortable, neatly ordered boats. The cost for the best ones would be about a dollar each per month. Should one desire extra rowers for an hour or a day, they can be hired for two or four cents.

THE HOUSEBOAT "DIANA" MOORED AT THE FOOT OF THE TAKHT-I-SULIEMAN

The "Diana," the largest houseboat on the Jhelum, is well appointed and beautifully furnished throughout. The turbaned figures are a few of the servants and boatmen of this floating home in the attitude of attention assumed whenever a picture was being taken or any other excuse was offered to take them from their tasks.

III

THE DIANA

*"Many a fair bark that all the day
Had lurked in sheltering creek or bay"*
Lalla Rookh.

THE Diana was called the pick of all the houseboats on the river, at least that is the way she was described by one of the residents in Srinagar before we had seen her. After visiting some fifty or more of the larger ones and later seeing all the handsome private boats, we could fully appreciate what he meant. She had been built by a man of rare and discriminating taste for his own private use, and as he had had a wide experience in houseboats he saw to it that nothing was omitted that could make her comfortable and attractive. Nor had she ever been rented until her owner's official duties called him to England and France.

The accompanying photographs will give some idea of her external appearance, though they do not do her justice, as she is a far finer looking boat than any of the pictures would indicate. One of her admirers said she had a very distinguished air and looked like a gentleman's boat—whatever that may mean. We were delighted with her and left her for our "hut" —that is what the cottages are called in Gulmarg—with real regret and were very glad to return to her again after an absence of two months in that deservedly popular summer resort. As will be seen from the photographs, she has two lower decks—one at each end—with a passageway running throughout her entire length on either side connecting these decks with one another, while above there is an upper deck with an awning and a number of easy chairs and tables. She is somewhat over a hundred feet long and about fourteen feet wide. The first room in front serves as an ante-room. It is of good size with a handsomely decorated ceiling and has charming stained-glass windows, with carved woodwork around the doors and openings. The furniture includes large brass-bound desks, chairs, Turkish rugs, pieces of damascened ware, shields and swords, and three water-color pictures.

The next room, about twice as large, is the drawing-room. This has a handsomely upholstered divan, three large easy chairs, brass-bound bookshelves, walnut rods with gold inlaid decorations, six small oil paintings, one artistic papier-mâché shelf, an elaborately carved mantel and overmantel at the fireplace, with a richly wrought brass fender and handsome brass-bound wood box, beautifully carved wood desk and table, carved wood decorations around the door openings, a large rich brass plate, a folding table, five large oil paintings, and two Turkish rugs. Back of this is the dining-room, which is about fourteen feet long and the same breadth as the other rooms. This has a mantel and fireplace like the drawing-room, with a very elaborately carved overmantel, on the top of which is a handsome brass piece. The sills of all the doors and windows are brass and there are brass-bound book-cases, a very large brass-bound sideboard, dining table and chairs, a brass-bound tea table, four oil paintings, a Turkish rug and Oriental curtains. In addition to these rooms there are three handsomely furnished bedrooms with open fireplaces, and two bathrooms. She is fitted up with the necessary housekeeping equipment for a family of eight or ten people and is entirely ready for occupancy.

A DOMESTIC RICE MILL

The charm of Kashmir is that it is distinctively itself. A walk through the bazaars, the huts and factories presents a living panorama of the India of the imagination. Here are to be seen the flashing colors, the turbaned heads and the picturesque groups of the populace at work and at play.

IV

THE SERVANTS

"On either side with ready hearts and hands,
His chosen guard of bold believers stands"
—*Lalla Rookh.*

THE servant problem is here just as elsewhere, only here service is less expensive. However, it is a very important consideration and should be settled as soon as a houseboat or cottage has been chosen. While we were in Bombay friends had told us such awful tales about the Kashmiri servants—that they were such liars and thieves—we decided to follow the advice they gave us as a result of their own experiences and take a bearer, or butler, and a cook from India, both of whom spoke English. It was in this way that we had the nucleus of our corps on our arrival.

In Srinagar we were advised to see the government official who had charge of this matter and hire all our servants through his office, as such servants would have to come with his approval and in case of trouble would be held responsible by him. We therefore engaged a bhisti—a water-carrier—a butler's assistant, a sweeper, two derseys, a dhobie, a cook's assistant, three men to act as grooms for the saddle-horses, and three boatmen. These constituted our regular force, but were supplemented from time to time by a variety of helpers as we required them.

The wages of our Indian butler and cook were about ten dollars each per month, but they provided all their own clothing and food, even when we were traveling. The bhisti received three dollars a month; the butler's assistant one dollar and sixty-six cents a month; the sweeper three dollars per month. The derseys received five dollars for the chief and three dollars and thirty-three cents for his assistant, these two men doing all the sewing and mending for the family, as well as making all sorts of articles of wearing apparel, including

THE VALE OF KASHMIR

suits of clothes, dresses and shirtwaists. The dhobie, or laundryman, had six dollars and sixty-six cents a month for doing all the laundry for the entire family of six persons, and as we wore white most of the time there were sometimes over a thousand pieces per month. The laundry was all taken away on Monday and returned on Saturday, and as a rule was remarkably well done.

The cook's assistant, who was a general errand boy as well, had a dollar and sixty-six cents per month. The wages of the three boatmen were included in the cost of the kitchen boat, as were those of the hostlers in the charges for the saddle-horses. We paid about eight dollars per month for each man and horse, though this price covered the cost for the use of the horse, his food and care, as well as the wages and food of the men, who slept with the horses. As these horses were from the Maharaja's stables they were supposed to be the best to be had in the Valley, and the men were held responsible by the Maharaja's officer who was in charge of his stables. Whenever a horse or man proved unsatisfactory a change was at once made. In addition to the above we also had a caddie boy for golf, who received two dollars per month, which also covered the cost of his food and clothes, and when he was not serving as caddie, he did anything else that might be required of him.

Then, too, when we went up or down the river, or had the position of our boat changed, we employed a small army of trackers, who towed the boat from the shore or pushed it along with poles as the occasion required. Naturally our force was somewhat larger than the average on account of the unusual size of the Diana, which, as we have already said, was one of the largest boats on the river.

I have mentioned that we brought the bearer and cook from India to avoid trouble and secure protection, but unfortunately we experienced the reverse. Very soon difficulties arose with the Kashmiri servants who did not like the "down country" men, as they were called. One day there was a

THE VALE OF KASHMIR

disgraceful row just outside the boat on the bank, which quieted down in a measure when I appeared with a switch. It was impossible to learn the facts, so I sent for the Maharaja's representative, who came with assistants and held a sort of court of inquiry. After he had carefully examined all the servants, the result of his investigation was summed up in the statement that the Kashmiri servants did not like my bearer. He said, however, he had threatened them all with fine and imprisonment if there was any further trouble. This had the result of keeping peace for a few days, but the bearer seemed to be afraid the Kashmiri servants might poison him or do him some violence, and asked to be released from his contract. After a little persuasion he consented to remain for a while longer and try it. But I was not surprised a few days later to have him come and say he must go the next day, and go he did.

We then engaged a Kashmiri bearer, who spoke English and had been trained in an English household, and, although he was one of the most highly paid bearers in the Valley, his wages were only six dollars and sixty-six cents per month, including food and clothes. He proved so competent and trustworthy that later on he became a sort of steward, having charge of all the other servants, making most of the purchases, and attending to all other arrangements in connection with our housekeeping. He acted as interpreter and saw to it that all the other servants did their work properly. During the Mohammedan fast he and all his co-religionists—and most of our servants were Mohammedans—fasted from dawn till after sunset with no falling off in the discharge of their duties. At certain hours Sultana—the bearer—held a sort of service with the others, and he told me that all were very faithful in the observance of this fast, which seemed remarkable as it lasted over a month.

Prior to this we had been compelled to let Rama, the cook, go. The parting came about in this manner: We were on our way up the river to Islamabad when I noticed that the bearer always went with the cook every time any purchases were made, but nothing was said until one day the cook was ill and Sultana came to me for instructions and advice. It then came out that the cook could not speak Kashmiri and that all the purchases had to be made by the bearer. When I asked how the cook had got on in Srinagar, I found that the merchants there understood Hindu, which was not the case in the villages along the river. As he had professed to understand and speak the native language he was a little disconcerted to have me make this discovery, and told me that his wife was very ill and that he must return to Bombay at once. After this Sultana made all the purchases and I found that the cost of our food decreased between fifteen and twenty per cent. This was another evidence of the ill-feeling toward the "down country" men on the part of the Kashmiri, who thought that these foreigners were holding places that should be filled by natives; for, curious as it may seem, these Indian servants were considered foreigners quite as much as we were, with this difference, that they liked us and disliked them. Moreover, I found to my surprise that I could have bought food in the bazaars by using a native interpreter for less than my Bombay cook could. This, however, was one of many interesting incidents in our Kashmiri educational experience.

Still another servant I have not mentioned, as we did not have him when we were in the houseboat, but during July and August, when we took the cottage in Gulmarg. For the want of a better name he might be called a woodman. Sultana had told me we should need another servant, but that he would be a great saving to me, because he would chop and provide all the wood that we used. This would be a large item as we had open fires in each room and they would be going almost continually, for, owing to the high altitude of eight thousand five hundred feet it was very cold indeed at times, especially at night. Then, too, we had several cooking stoves in the kitchen to be provided with wood. How much we actually burned I do not know, but it must have been a good many

A PRIMITIVE SUSPENSION BRIDGE AT URI

This swing bridge, known as *jhula*, is made of twisted birch twigs and spans the river below the fort at Uri. When the river is high the middle of the bridge touches the water, and at all times it requires a steady head and acrobatic muscular development.

cords, all of which cost for the entire two months we were there the vast sum of four dollars, that being the woodman's wages, and it should not be forgotten that he, like all the other servants, provided all his own food and clothing. It is hard to understand how these servants can live on such wages and rear families, and yet they do and save money besides.

There were other servants, in addition to these purely domestic ones, but it is only necessary to say that their wages were all on the same low scale. For instance, in Gulmarg if one wished to economize in the matter of horses a good-sized pony and hostler could be had for five dollars a month, instead of eight, and this included the services of the man and food for both man and beast. It will be seen from the foregoing that the cost of living, as far as servants are concerned, is very light, but it should not be forgotten that these are prices paid by a temporary resident, while those paid by permanent residents are very much less. For instance, a native bearer would only cost three dollars and thirty-three cents to four dollars a month, if he did not speak English—and as a rule the best ones do not. And the bhistis and sweepers would only receive from two dollars to two dollars and thirty-three cents per month, while all others are proportionately low. Nor are these rates likely to increase very much, as the Valley is so comparatively difficult of access that rich, extravagant and pleasure-loving tourists are not inclined to take the long and, to some, very fatiguing journey necessary to reach Srinagar. And yet I have known, as stated elsewhere, a number of visitors, who were upward of seventy years of age, who had not only made this journey but thoroughly enjoyed it.

V
FOODS

"The board was spread with fruits and wine;
With grapes of gold, like those that shine
On Casbin's hills;" —*Lalla Rookh*.

A QUESTION of almost equal importance to that of servants is that of food, and it is a gratifying surprise to find that most things one is accustomed to at home can be had here, though some, it is true, are imported in tins. The number of fresh vegetables, however, is remarkably large when you consider that the natives look upon rice as the principal article of food. These fresh vegetables can be bought in the bazaars, or from market boats, or from private farms, or from Nedou, the hotel proprietor, or at times from the Club, which, as stated elsewhere, has its own kitchen garden. While the prices vary somewhat in the different sources of supply, they are all low when compared to charges at home. Nor are the prices of imported foods as high as one would expect, when it is remembered that some of them come from Europe to India and have a rail haul to Rawal Pindi and a two weeks' wagon cartage into Srinagar. Meats of various kinds are to be had, with the exception of beef, and the reason this is rarely had is due largely to the fact that the Maharaja is a Hindu and holds the cow as a sacred object. To kill one is illegal, though the temptation is not great to the average European as the cattle one sees are, for the most part, small, ill-favored and bony. The only really good stock belongs to private individuals and is kept for the milk and butter. Lamb and mutton are excellent, abundant and cheap. There is also a good supply of fish, there being some delicious trout to be found in the mountain streams. Then, too, there is a fairly good supply of game at certain seasons.

One thing, however, should always be borne in mind, and that is that the natives are very negligent about what Occidentals consider necessary sanitary precautions. This is a very

A FOOD BAZAAR

While the income of the native is very small, the purchasing power of his money is extraordinary. Here eggs are 4 to 8 cents per dozen; good-sized chickens 10 cents each; ducks 4 cents; rice 2 cents per pound; milk less than 3 cents a quart; and other staples in like ratio.

THE VALE OF KASHMIR

serious matter, as enteric diseases are common and at times dangerous; and even serious cholera epidemics have come in the past, though there has been a great improvement in this respect since the introduction of running water, which can be had from numerous taps in all parts of the city. Great care, too, is exercised in watching the sources of water supply, the condition of the reservoir and the taps from which the water is drawn. It is, however, a curious and striking fact that so strong is the force of inherited habit, that is if a habit can be inherited, that many of the natives, whose ancestors have been accustomed for centuries to drink the water from the river, still prefer this, which is at times little better than modified sewerage. Near our houseboat was a flight of steps to the river, and there must have been forty or fifty girls and women water-carriers who came there every day, all of whom had to pass two taps on the way and this was but one of hundreds of similar places. Nor do these natives take the trouble to boil the water before drinking it, though many of them let it stand in a brass or copper jar, and this is said to make it comparatively safe. For Occidentals, however, there are certain rules that should be invariably followed. The water, no matter where it comes from, should be boiled, and so should the milk. The greatest care should be exercised in eating butter, which it is better to let alone unless you are perfectly certain about it. Salads, or any vegetables that are to be eaten raw, should be washed in boiled water and all uncooked or raw fruits should be carefully washed. Finally, it is a wise precaution to be inoculated for enteric, as the percentage of cases of enteric on the part of people who have been inoculated is so slight as to be inconsiderable. This, however, it is a good thing to do in any Oriental country. I know of one family consisting of parents and four young daughters who were traveling for nearly two years in countries where enteric diseases were not only common, but frequently fatal, and yet, because they had been inoculated, they never had the slightest difficulty.

THE VALE OF KASHMIR

But in order that some idea of the cost of the principal articles of food may be had, the following list is given: Twelve average-size loaves of bread cost only 33 cents; six pounds of good mutton about the same; good-sized chickens, 20 cents a pair; ducks, from 4 to 6 cents each, and 10 to 14 cents in summer when the Valley is crowded with visitors and the demand quadrupled for many things; geese, large and fine ones, 30 cents; fish, 3 to 5 cents for two pounds; eggs, from 4 to 8 cents a dozen; milk, less than 3 cents a quart; potatoes, about 1½ cents a pound, and other vegetables at similar prices; apples, 25 cents a hundred; pears, 8 and 10 cents a hundred; melons, 2 to 4 cents apiece; apricots and peaches, 2 cents a pound; rice, 2 cents a pound; flour, 3 or 4 cents a pound.

Many of the more particular residents have their own private sources of supply of milk, and Nedou, the hotel keeper, has an especially fine herd from which he provides for his hotel and a large number of his personal friends and patrons who are in houseboats. The large majority, however, depend upon the natives and the native sources of supply that come, in some instances, quite a number of miles. This milk is brought in jars that are carried on the heads of the milkmen, who, as a rule, come from their villages in companies of from six to twenty or thirty.

Perhaps no sight impresses the visitor for the first time more forcibly than the appearance of one of these companies of twenty or thirty, as they trot on their way to deliver this milk. As a rule they start on a trot and trot as long as they can, then stop to rest, putting the jars in some stream of water to keep cool. As soon as they are rested and get their breath they start again, and this continues over a distance sometimes from ten to twenty miles. Of course it sometimes happens that on hot days this milk changes its character and consistency very much, and as these jars are washed with the indifference of native care, the blending and mingling of microbes must be a severe tax on the Kashmiri stomach.

A CAMPERS' PARADISE—A VIEW IN THE CHENAR BAGH

The rudely thatched native boats in the foreground are the only homes known by thousands of the natives, while the tent and dungah boat under the shade of the chenar tree is one of the many visitors' camps that line these shores during the summer.

VI

FINDING A PLACE

"Then, the sounds from the lake—the low whispering in boats,
As they shoot through the moonlight;—the dipping of oars"
—*Lalla Rookh.*

ONCE you have selected your houseboat and the necessary servants have been engaged, it is well to decide upon a place on the river as soon as possible, or, if not on the river, in one of the canals, or perhaps on the Dhal Lake. Where this shall be is largely a matter of taste and convenience. A portion of the bank is reserved for boats using electric lights, and any boats not fitted up in this way must move on, no matter how long they may have been in place. This is a very important thing to know, as it is extremely unpleasant to be compelled to move once you have become comfortably and satisfactorily settled. Several of whom we heard were greatly annoyed by being forced to change after they had been tied up for several weeks in a delightful spot, simply because some new arrival had rented a boat fitted for electricity and wished that place. Therefore, if your own boat is not fitted for electricity and you have chosen an anchorage in this portion of the bank, you may have a visit from the policeman at any time, and receive an official notice that the place you are occupying is required by a boat having electric lights. They are very polite about it and full of apologies for troubling you, but such is the rule and they are merely doing what the law requires. It is well, therefore, if you have a boat that is not fitted up for electricity, to avoid this very desirable section of the bank and to choose a place where you are not too far from the Club and other centers of interest. You should make your choice with due regard to quiet, as some of the landings are very noisy, especially when near a cluster of native houses. The verbal battles that take place, as well as the parental administrations of discipline to disobedient offspring, mingled with the babble of bargaining and the barking and howling of fighting dogs, are not conducive to an amiable frame of mind. There are, however, a large number of delightful places, though some of them are a little remote from the Club.

Another important consideration is shade. While there are many large shade trees along both banks, certain places are so popular that when one of them is given up, there are several applicants prepared to take immediate possession, and often it is purely a question of which boat can get there first. These struggles frequently take place in the early morning and the first intimation the occupants of the boat have as to what is going on is to be sharply awakened from a sound slumber by a collision with another boat, and the attendant violent vocal warfare that ensues. But when the first flush of excitement is over, the result is accepted in the best of good grace. These servants who were squabbling violently a few minutes ago are now fraternizing, eating and smoking together like the best of friends.

There is, then, a wide choice in the matter of a place, and, while the river banks are very popular, some of the delightfully shaded canals and the Dhal Lake have their staunch adherents, who wax eloquent in describing their advantages over the river sites.

Still another important consideration is your neighbors. For if they are congenial, each day is a delight. Of course, old comers, who have been summering in the Valley for many years, have the best of it, as they not only know one another very well, but understand just what to do without any loss of time.

VII

THE PICTURESQUE RIVER

*"Where melted all to form the stream;
And here fair islets, small and bright"*
—*Lalla Rookh.*

TRAVELERS who are keenly sensitive to the beautiful and the picturesque are all agreed that it would be difficult, if not impossible, to find another stretch of river scenery and life to equal in these respects that of the Jhelum, and the more extensive their travels have been the more certain does this conviction become. Many esteem a sail through the Grand Canal and other canals of Venice to offer one of the most picturesque delights it would be possible to have, but even Venice must yield in some respects to the Jhelum where it flows through the city of Srinagar. This river throughout its course is very winding—so much so that in a journey of eighty miles by river the distance by road is only sixty miles—and these windings are very much sharper and more numerous in certain parts of the river than in others.

The city is built on both banks of the river, and a more interesting combination of buildings of all kinds and descriptions it would be impossible to find. So great is this variety that a daily sail through the seven miles, or under the seven bridges that cross the river at different points, for eight months never fails to interest and delight.

In the upper part of the city the banks are lined with houseboats in which the visitors live. But lower down these banks, which are sometimes twenty and thirty feet high, have a very interesting and varied life at the water's edge, where you find laundrymen and laundrywomen at intervals all the way along, and bathers, sometimes composed of groups of men, others of groups of women, and again men and women together. As a rule this bathing takes place at the foot of some of the wide stone steps that lead up from the water to

THE VALE OF KASHMIR

the upper level of the bank, and frequently in the vicinity of a temple or mosque. There are also a number of small bath-houses, without roofs, and divided into very tiny little cabinets that are hardly large enough for a single person. These are indulged in by the more fortunate, or the better-to-do classes, who constitute but a very small percentage of the total bathing population.

This bathing, too, is a very interesting process to witness, especially the dressing, for, while the men are rather indifferent as to how much or how little clothing they may have on, the women are exceedingly modest and rarely, if ever, is there the least exposure of any portion of the body besides the arms, and head and feet. They go into the river with one dress on and when they have bathed they have not only washed their bodies but the garments they have been wearing, and when they come out they have on the bank, or steps, another garment which they put on, and so skillful are they in making this change that it is almost impossible to tell how it is done. One moment they are clad in the wet, clinging clothes which they have worn in the river, and the next by a rapid sleight-of-hand transformation they are dressed in dry garments of most pleasing hue.

Another interesting feature that is to be seen at frequent intervals along the bank is what is called "beating out the rice," and this is sometimes done by little children, and at other times by quite old men and women. There is a large wooden or earthen jar in which the rice is put, and on either side the beaters stand holding a sort of pole, and they bend over and pound down on the rice until it has been entirely hulled. Some of the little girls who do this are so graceful and so pretty that they form a most attractive picture.

Then, too, there is a lot of business done by vegetable dealers and fruit venders and merchants of all sorts along the river's edge, while above rise the buildings, some quite new and attractive, and others apparently held up by poles. These sometimes rise one almost on top of the other clear to the highest

Seen from the Takht, the Jhelum winds its torturous course like a great silver serpent through the Valley. There is no more inspiring view to be had than from this mountain.

The River Jhelum and the canals that connect with it form the high roads for all the activities of the people, and a sail over these waters presents an ever-changing panorama of Oriental life.

THE VALE OF KASHMIR

elevation of the bank. Some seem to be on the point of falling into the river, and nearly all have open balconies that are really living-rooms which project far beyond the front of the buildings and well over the edge of the bank, and occasionally these do fall into the river.

This jumble of picturesque buildings that have no especial relation to one another and form a constantly varying mass throughout all the seven miles, are animated, at least as far as the windows and balconies are concerned, by the dwellers, who are sometimes sewing, sometimes weaving, sometimes cooking, sometimes reading or smoking, and very frequently gossiping. Nor are they ever so busy that they cannot pause to watch the boats of the visitors as they pass by, for Europeans and foreigners are just as interesting to them as they are to foreigners.

Moreover, this sail on the river takes you past all of the principal palaces of the Maharaja and his ministers, as well as the so-called European shops, that are kept for the most part by natives or Parsees, and it is in this way that much of the shopping is done by the dwellers in the houseboats, for every houseboat has its own kitchen boat and its own rowboat, which as a rule is a very comfortable affair, arranged with awnings and curtains to protect you from the sun and the glare on the river, with the rowers at either end. The rowers are really paddlers, as there is practically no rowing done, except by the students in the schools, where oars are used.

It is therefore a fascinating and interesting experience to sail all the way down under the seven different bridges, each of which has its own picturesque features and character. This is also the best way to reach certain parts of the city, because you avoid the narrow and filthy streets, and by landing at a point near the shops you wish to visit, it is very easy to reach almost any portion of the city.

Another interesting feature of the river life is the water-carrier, and the water-carrier may be either a man or a woman and either young or old. The men for the most part carry skins that are filled with water, while the women carry jugs, and some of these jugs that the little girls bear are almost a third of their own height. It is astonishing how cleverly they fill them and then place them on their heads and balance them as they climb the steps. Their indifference to sanitary matters is also indicated in the way in which this is done. A woman, or several women, as these water-carriers frequently go about in groups, will descend to the river's edge and there they will wash their hands and faces and feet, and almost at the same moment fill their jugs with the water in which they have been bathing.

These features are only a few of the almost infinite variety that goes to make up the setting of the river life, while above and beyond are the splendid chenar trees. Rising higher still in the distance, is the magnificent mountain wall. In the upper part of the river where it is pretty wide and the banks are free from buildings and beautifully wooded, it is quite customary for the dwellers in the houseboats to put up tents and camp there for a season. This sort of camp life is often very charming, especially about afternoon tea-time, when people are calling on and entertaining one another.

Still farther up the river the houseboats become less frequent, and while there are some beautiful homes embowered in flowers and shade trees, it is much quieter, although with the exception of July and August even this portion of the river presents a very animated picture, especially in the latter part of the afternoon.

There are of course some phases of the life on the river that are less attractive than others, as for instance the fact that the river is treated by the natives as a sort of glorified sewer and all sorts of filth are emptied into it, and it not infrequently happens that you see a dead dog, or a dead cow, or a dead chicken go floating by your houseboat. Fortunately these unattractive and rather gruesome features are comparatively rare.

BEATING OUT THE RICE

The roll of centuries has left but little impress upon many of the customs of the people of this remote Valley. This typical scene on the banks of the River Jhelum is the same today as it was centuries ago.

THE VALE OF KASHMIR

I have spoken chiefly of the river life in so far as it concerns the city itself and shall reserve anything that may be said beyond this for other chapters, especially the one devoted to Islamabad.

VIII

THE DHAL LAKE

> "Oh! to see it at sunset, when warm o'er the lake
> Its splendor at parting a summer eve throws"
> —*Lalla Rookh.*

THERE is probably no one name that one hears more frequently mentioned than the Dhal Lake, and my impression is that there was hardly a day during our eight months in the Valley that passed without some allusion being made to this fascinating body of water. This is due to the fact that it is a favorite place for picnics and excursions and campers, so that people are coming and going almost constantly and the chances are that in the course of a day one would meet a number of people who would either ask if you were going to the Dhal Lake today, or tell you that they or some of their friends had been or were going, or that some special function was to take place there or on its shores.

And it is well worthy of all the attention it receives, as it never fails to delight and is remembered with the greatest pleasure. As stated elsewhere, one of the finest views of this Lake is to be had from the Takht-i-Suleiman, and one realizes at the first glance that what is called a lake is in reality a combination of canals, rivers, various bodies of water, and marshes. Probably this interesting variety has much to do with its great charm. It is not a very extensive body of water, being but five miles long and about two miles wide, and while in places it is shallow and inclined to be marshy, in other places it is very deep. But everywhere the water is as clear as crystal and one sees the bottom in most parts with perfect distinctness.

Possibly the most striking feature associated with the Lake is the wonderful mountain amphitheater that rises on three sides beyond it to a height of from three to four thousand feet above the water. On the ground at the foot of these

THE NISHAT BAGH ON DHAL LAKE

During the time of the Delhi Emperors some of these great Moguls used Kashmir as their playground and summer residence, surrounding themselves with everything that was luxurious and beautiful. These exquisite gardens, now belonging to the Maharaja, give the traveler a glimpse into Kashmir's romantic past.

THE VALE OF KASHMIR

mountains and at the edge of the Lake there are many villages that are frequently surrounded by orchards, and, as already stated, several very renowned gardens that were constructed by the famous Delhi Emperors.

Towards the west it is open and flat and it is here that you find the curious floating gardens—gardens that are made of earth and vegetable matter accumulated on water plants. So prominent a feature are these gardens that possibly a few words in regard to them may not be amiss. The natives collect a certain kind of weed that has a great deal of air in the roots and tie these together in strips, each of which is about four feet broad and twenty to thirty feet long, and sometimes they will extend them so that they look like huge vegetable rafts floating on the surface of the water. On these a certain amount of earth is placed in which the seeds are planted. It is quite wonderful what choice and large melons, cucumbers, tomatoes, eggplants, etc., are raised, as all of these seem to grow most luxuriantly with comparatively little care and are a source of important revenue to the natives. Occasionally, however, they meet with what is almost in the nature of disaster, for a strong wind or heavy storm will tear them to pieces and scatter them all over the surface of the Lake, with the result that all the labor and all the fruit is lost. In order that one may realize the extent of these floating gardens, it has been estimated that if they could be brought together, it would probably make an area several miles square. As it is, one sees them here and there, in all parts of the Lake, especially in protected bays where they are less liable to destruction.

In this direction, too, there is a sort of half-reclaimed marsh, that alternates with strips of shallow water, and beyond this the city itself. As already stated, the Dhal is not one sheet of water, but is divided by causeways and projecting marshland into three different portions, and it is in parts so covered with aquatic plants that comparatively little water is to be seen by the end of summer. Going up the Nasim Bagh in a small boat, it takes about an hour from the Dhal gate

THE VALE OF KASHMIR

to the Lake. At first the canal passes between small fields and orchards, but after traveling about a mile, the village of Renawari is passed. To the left one notices a temple that stands far out into the water, and close by this is a landing-place where much of the lake produce is sold. Continuing on the picturesque canal through the village you soon come to the three-arch stone bridge which crosses the canal. There the canal branches, one portion turning to the left. This is called the Cadal Mullah and on its banks you notice an old ruined mosque, called Hassanabad, which has the distinction of being one of the very few stone mosques in Kashmir. Near by are many of the graves of the kings and nobles of the thirteenth and fourteenth centuries. Soon after this the canal spreads out into a series of wide lakelets that extend around the foot of Hari Parbat.

The main canal goes straight on through groves of willow and gardens and wide open spaces alternately for about two miles before opening into the Lake. On the edge of the Lake there is a village with a large mosque called Harzrat Bal, because of the supposed hair of the prophet which is said to be kept there and shown on certain days, when fully half the city gathers to see it. A little further on is the Nasim Bagh. This is a fine park-like expanse, closely planted with magnificent chenar trees and rises so high above the Lake that it catches the breezes and thence its name. During the early summer months this is considered the most delightful encampment on the Lake and several yachts have been built in recent years. Others have chosen this spot for camping on account of the sailing advantages it offers, and occasionally some regattas have been held. Unfortunately much of the masonry and foundations of the terraces have been destroyed, but the trees are at their best, and no more exquisite view of the open expanse of the Lake and the splendid snow-crowned top of Mahadev is to be had anywhere than that from under the dense shade of these noble trees.

THE VALE OF KASHMIR

In the middle of this part of the Lake is the so-called Char Chenar Island, which is an artificial island about forty yards square. After passing the Nasim Bagh you come to a village and some large houses, not far from which is an oil factory. At this corner of the Lake the River Telbal flows in. Up this boats can go for nearly two miles, and it is not only exceedingly pretty, but there is excellent fishing to be had and the water is intensely cold. About a mile to the east of this is the canal of the Shalimar Gardens, which are about a mile in length. The Shali Bagh, as the Kashmiri call it, is a large walled enclosure on sloping ground at the foot of the narrow valley which emerges here from the hills that encircle the Lake. The terraces have been planted with orchards and chenar trees, and the banks are bordered by an avenue on either side, while at the end of each terrace a summer-house flanks the waterfalls. There is a fine fall on the upper terrace that is quite surrounded by water and fountains, and the pillars of the veranda are made of polished marble brought from Pampur. The upper part of the garden, the name of which means "Abode of Love," was set apart for the Emperor's Zenana, and it is well worthy of Jehangir's fair Queen, Nur Mahal, to whose taste and love of beautiful scenery the Mughal Gardens in Kashmir bear eloquent witness. A few years ago there was a banquet given on the King's birthday at the Shalimar Bagh, and the scene on this occasion is said to have been very weird and fascinating because of the glitter of the myriad of lamps that illumined the beautiful dresses and fair faces, and the play and splash of the fountains blended with the singing of the dancers. There is a heronry on one side of the garden.

After leaving the Shalimar Bagh you come to the Nishat Bagh, passing under a stone bridge on the way where the Sutoo crosses the Lake and then enters the middle and its longest portion. Just in front of the bridge is the Nishat Bagh, or "Garden of Gladness," the terraces of which cover the steep slopes of the hill. Fronting the Lake there is a large house and after this a series of terraces, of waterfalls and

THE VALE OF KASHMIR

fountains that play on Sundays and festal occasions. On the upper platform there are some stately chenar trees and the waterfalls are of considerable height. The highest elevation is far above the Lake, which it commands and of which there is a glorious view across the Valley. This is considered by many to be the most charming spot on the Lake and is very popular with picnickers, as it has the advantage of being comparatively near the Shalimar Bagh. Coming back from the Nishat Bagh the boat traverses the whole length of the Lake, near the middle of which in this portion is the Rupa Lanka, an artificial island with a few small trees. About half way between this and the Takht there is a narrow strait through which you enter the southern part of the Lake. There is no more delightful horseback ride in the Valley of Kashmir than the bridle-path which leads around the edge of the Takht, as well as that which commands the waters of the Lake from time to time through vistas in the trees. It is in this general direction that some of the most delightful country houses, with their beautiful gardens, are to be seen, all of which are usually occupied in the summer months by European visitors.

ONE OF THE SEVEN BRIDGES THAT SPAN THE JHELUM RIVER

The River Jhelum is the main artery of traffic through the City of Srinagar. Its banks are lined on each side by shops and bazaars of every nature, and the teeming multitude crossing its seven bridges, together with the unbroken procession on the river, presents a sight of unfailing interest.

IX

SHOPS AND BAZAARS

*"All were abroad—the busiest hive
On Bela's hills is less alive"*
—*Lalla Rookh.*

THE shops contribute largely to the comfort of the visitors and residents, because in them are to be found all of the European supplies in the way of clothing and foods and materials of various kinds, as very few of these imported articles are to be had in the native bazaars. Many of these shops, as stated elsewhere, are kept by Parsees, or natives of the more important class, though a few belong to Europeans, but the articles to be found at each are very much alike. For the convenience of visitors most of them are located along the river bank and some are large and well stocked, being somewhat like a small department store. It is in this section, too, that the Punjab Bank is to be found, and it is a very busy place on certain days and at certain times during the month, for, while there are other banks, or business houses that do a little banking, this is the chief financial center and has a branch in Gulmarg during the summer season.

When one considers the long distances imported articles have to be carried in the bullock carts over the mountain passes, it is surprising what a variety is to be found in these shops and how excellent is the quality. Naturally the prices for imported articles are considerably higher than those of similar articles to be found in the native bazaars and many who desire to economize patronize the latter very largely and only buy in the shops what they cannot find in the bazaars.

These bazaars, like nearly all Oriental bazaars, are very picturesque and interesting, especially during the first visit. But if one goes frequently, the dirt and smells and crowds and general insanitary condition of some of the narrow streets become offensive. They are very numerous, however, and stretch for some miles on either bank of the river or on the streets that run back from the river and parallel with the river. Indeed most of these streets are lined with bazaars, which sometimes open into the side streets or ramify off in other directions. They are patronized chiefly by the natives and the scene around certain of them, made up as it is of men and women and children, all endeavoring to make the best bargain they can (the shopkeeper trying to get as high a price as possible and the purchaser to give as low a sum as he can get the article for), is frequently a very animated one. Indeed, a peaceful tourist might think a diminutive riot is going on. At these bazaars, which are all open to the street and display their wares practically on the street, are to be found all sorts of native products and some imported articles, such as cotton cloths, watches and certain kinds of hardware.

The bazaars where food is sold are always very crowded at certain hours of the day, and it is surprising to find how much cheaper some articles can be bought here than in the shops. But one does not feel much inclined to buy such articles as rice, flour, meal, sugar and salt after he has seen them handled and poked by the natives and witnessed the swarms of flies that light on them and come from them. These facts, however, do not seem to disturb the natives themselves in the very slightest degree.

The shops where carved furniture, silver, bronzes and brasses are to be found are for the most part in private houses, or what have been private houses and changed into shops. The tailors, however—and there are a great many of them—have shops in the bazaars, and these are frequently, like the bazaars themselves, open to the street, although the more important ones that cater to European trade have arranged rooms in the rear of the front where their goods are to be seen in greater privacy and where the measurements are taken and the garments are tried on. At some of these it is quite surprising to find such excellent materials, and even more so to see how well the garments are cut and made, especially if the purchaser

A CANDY KITCHEN OF KASHMIR

Wild honey and almond paste form the main ingredients of a large variety of confections that are very delicious and are held in high esteem by the natives. The candy kitchens are popular meeting places where the news and gossip of the day are exchanged.

THE VALE OF KASHMIR

has a garment of a certain style that he can give the tailor as a sample. One of these men, for instance, has a cutter who was taught, or learned his trade, in a London shop where there were many American patrons; and some of the garments made by this tailor are so well cut and shaped that it is impossible to realize, or to believe, that they have not come from London, or Paris, or New York.

More astonishing, however, than all else, and seemingly incredible to many, is the cost of these articles. For instance, one gentleman had a suit of homespun that had been made in America and for which he had paid eighty dollars. As this was getting a little old he asked one of the tailors if it would be possible to get any more cloth like it. The tailor said: "Certainly, I can get you some exactly like that." The gentleman asked how long it would take, and was told about three weeks. The gentleman exclaimed: "What! is this possible? How can you get cloth out from England in so short a time as that?" "Oh!" the tailor replied, "it would not be brought out from England. It would be made here." "What!" the gentleman questioned, "can cloth like this be made here in Kashmir?" "Yes," said the tailor, "and if it is not satisfactory you need not take it. The only thing necessary will be to loan me one of your garments so that I can give it to the weaver who will make the cloth."

This was done and in less than a month a piece of cloth large enough for a couple of suits of clothes was shown the gentleman, and so nearly like his own was the material that it was almost impossible to distinguish one from the other, the only difference being in favor of the native product, which seemed somewhat nicer in quality. This suit of clothes was made and lined with silk, there being three garments—a coat, waistcoat and trousers—and when it was finished it fitted just as well as the suit that he had been wearing. For this suit of clothes, made of cloth that had been especially woven for him and lined with an excellent quality of silk, he paid only the equivalent of a little more than six dollars as against eighty dollars. His

THE VALE OF KASHMIR

wife was so pleased with this experiment that she took the balance of the cloth and had it made into a dress that would have cost her at least a hundred and fifty dollars at home, and for which she paid seven dollars.

And what is true of this suit is true of all the clothes and cloth made in the Valley by the natives, and though it really seems incredible that such could be the case, it is an absolute fact. These, however, represent the expensive and extravagant suits, as a homespun suit without silk lining could be bought for from between three and four dollars, and with such suits a cap, or hat of some sort is made of the same material without charge.

A STRIKING EXAMPLE OF THE KASHMIRI'S SKILL IN WOOD-CARVING

This is a two-panel section of a four-panel screen that was made to order by wood-carvers of Kashmir. The side of the screen shown in the illustration carries the Lhassa design, the reverse side being carved in the Kashmiri design of flowers, leaves and vines.

X

WOOD-CARVING AND SILVERWARE

> "In Fairy-land, whose streets and towers
> Are made of gems and light and flowers"
> —*Lalla Rookh.*

PROBABLY nothing is more surprising to the visitor than the wonderful beauty of the wood-carving that is done here, and his surprise is all the greater because the chances are that he has heard little or nothing about it before coming to the Valley. The writer by chance met a British officer just before going to Kashmir who in a measure prepared him for what he would find. He had been speaking of the carving and the screens in Egypt and regretted that he had not bought one of these, when this British officer said: "Well, you needn't, because you can get something far more beautiful and far less expensive in Kashmir." So one of the earliest visits he made after settling in the Valley was to these wood-carvers.

Here we found, as indicated in a former chapter, that houses had been turned into warerooms by the carvers for the display of their goods and some of the rooms were crowded with natives engaged in doing the carving itself. This is of so beautiful and delicate a character that one hesitates to attempt to describe it, even in the simplest way, for fear of appearing to exaggerate, and yet one who is familiar with this work realizes that it would be impossible to do this, so remarkable are these specimens of wood-carving. The present Queen of England was so impressed by them that at the time of her visit to the Durbar in India she ordered a large number of pieces, some of which were made from designs that she herself composed, merely selecting details from their own designs and so combining them so as to suit her wishes and tastes. This, however, any purchaser can do, as it is merely a matter of giving the dealer an idea of the kind of piece of furniture you

THE VALE OF KASHMIR

wish and then choosing from the great variety of designs those that you prefer.

The favorite designs, however, are called the Lhassa and the Kashmiri. In the former the dragon and animals prevail, and in the latter flowers and vines and leaves. A visit to these shops is a great treat to any lover of beautiful work, and the skill and cleverness shown in meeting the wishes of purchasers is very great. Moreover, these articles can be made to order and shipped to America with such care that comparatively little damage is done. Of course there is a certain amount of breakage, notwithstanding this care, but the writer had a large number of pieces made and the proportion of damage was comparatively slight and the repairs were readily made by a carpenter, not a wood-carver, here in America.

A very satisfactory arrangement for a visitor or purchaser to make is to select the articles he wishes as soon as he arrives in the Valley and have them made of such sizes and forms as suit the room in which he wishes to place them at home, and then use these articles in his own cottage or houseboat during his stay. Of course, if they are of a very elaborate character and they cannot be found already made, it may require some time—indeed, certain of the articles, like the more elaborate four-fold screens that have the Lhassa design on one side and the Kashmiri on the other, might require possibly a year to make. But these can be made, and will be if the purchaser so desires, with his own crest and his own coat-of-arms, so that they will have that measure of added individuality introduced in such a way as to seem a perfectly natural part of the design.

There are a number of men who do this work, all of whom are good, but it is well to visit them all and to place one's orders with the dealer who is most highly recommended by reliable residents. The writer himself had his articles made by three different men, and the only difficulty lay in insisting upon the fulfilment of the contract exactly as made. The pic-

THE ARTIZAN OF KASHMIR COMBINES UTILITY WITH BEAUTY OF FORM AND EXQUISITE DESIGN

The articles here shown illustrate the infinite capacity for taking pains, manifest in all the work of these artizans. Three designs are generally followed, the Lhassa as shown by the desk and large chair, the Kashmiri used on the chair to the left, and the Kashmir shawl design of the candlesticks and letterbox on the desk.

SEVERAL INTERESTING EXAMPLES OF WOOD-CARVING AND ENGRAVING ON SILVER

Top of cigar box, especially made for the Author; Queen Mary jewel box, the design of which was selected by Her Majesty, and another reproduction of which is shown on the cover of this volume; silver cigarette box, card case, purse and bon-bon box which are engraved with the Kashmir shawl design.

THE VALE OF KASHMIR

tures will give some idea of the grace and beauty of the articles as well as the designs and the workmanship.

This wood-carving has a possible rival in the silverwork that is done here, much of which is of very great beauty, and frequently the same dealer will have a silverware department, so that you can choose from the quaint and interesting designs or samples the figures or forms that have the most satisfyingly beautiful lines. One of the unusual samples is the adaptation of the beggar's bowl for table use. The designs that are engraved, of course, vary with the tastes of the purchaser, but the favorite design to be found here is that of the Kashmir shawl, and the tea sets and various articles that are engraved with this design are very charming and very delicate in their loveliness.

This ware, like the wood-carving, is comparatively inexpensive, somewhat more expensive than the foods and clothing, it is true, but the cost is very low compared with what such articles would bring in Europe or America, especially the latter.

Another ware that is to be found in these shops is papier-mâché work, and this is made in candlesticks, vases, boxes, paper holders, and paper knives, in fact a very wide variety of articles. The decorations for the most part are in design and color like those of the beautiful old Kashmir shawls, some being very delicate and subdued, and others bolder and stronger and more effective, but all rich and beautiful.

XI

NATIVE INDUSTRIES

> "When maids began to lift their heads,
> Refresh'd, from their embroidered beds"
> —*Lalla Rookh.*

UNDER this heading I wish to speak of the silk factory, which is a large and flourishing organization and employs four thousand men, women and children. This is a very ancient industry in the Valley, but it has only quite recently been brought to its present stage of perfect development, for the factory is said to be one of the best equipped silk factories in the world. The product of the looms is of a very high grade and forms an important factor in the output of the Valley. To provide the silk, of course, the cultivation of the mulberry and the silkworm is very general in different parts of the Valley. It has been stated by an authority in these matters that this factory is the largest of its kind in the world, and is heated and lighted by electric power. It is entirely under European supervision and the output has increased each year until between one and two hundred thousand pounds of raw silk are now being turned out. Besides this, in one year over twelve hundred men who are spread over the Valley took silkworm eggs from the factory and brought in their cocoons, receiving nearly two lakhs of rupees for their six weeks' labor. Weaving silk on hand-looms has also been started on a small scale experimentally. This silk factory is open to visitors on any morning and is one of the really interesting things to see.

There is also, as elsewhere stated, a very successful carpet factory. The Scottish proprietor when he came to Srinagar some years ago found a small effort of this kind being made, and has simply developed it until it has reached its present large proportions. There was no attempt made to change the ideas or the designs or the methods of weaving, but to improve

CHILDREN OF KASHMIR WEAVING RUGS

In the rug-making industry, which is the life-work of many of the natives from generation to generation, the entire family work at the looms, from the tiny tots, whose inborn skill needs little training, to the old grandfather whose bent form still hovers over the task that has held him and his fathers before him.

THE VALE OF KASHMIR

them wherever this was possible, and so all that is good that has been inherited from the past in the way of color and designs and workmanship has been retained and made more successful because the work is being done under more favorable conditions. A visit to this factory is another of the really interesting things to be done.

When you first enter the grounds, you are taken to a room where the designing is done, and are struck by the fact that several of the designers seem to have hair and beards of a peculiar and unnatural shade of red. When you ask why it is that so many of them are like this and inquire if it happens to be a family characteristic, you are told no, that it is simply because these men have become gray, or that their hair is white, and they don't like to look old and so they stain their hair and beards this peculiar shade of red, which happens to be the fashionable color with them at the present time.

These men show you the designs that they have made on paper, some of which are in black and white and others are in color, and when these designs have been finished they are taken in sections to the loom and given to the weaver. If one man is to complete the rug, which is usually the case, he has all of the different sections numbered and arranged in order, so that he can start his rug and by consulting his design, which is beside him, go on and complete it without any difficulty whatever.

This carpet factory is not, like the silk factory, in a modern and fine brick building, but is just a series of small wooden sheds such as have been used for a great many years, only they have been made as comfortable and as sanitary as the conditions will permit. In each of these sheds there may be several looms and the loom will be tended by one or two, or more, according to the size of the rug. It is of course very interesting to go from loom to loom and see the rugs in their different stages of development. When this has been done and visits have been made to the dyeing department—a very important one, for almost everything depends upon the quality

THE VALE OF KASHMIR

of the dye and the tones of the colors—the visitor is taken to the warehouse and shown a large number, if he chooses to see them, of the completed products; some of these are small rugs a few feet square, while others are practically carpets, twenty or thirty feet square. In fact almost any size of rug can be made that is desired and orders are received from England and elsewhere for rugs to cover entire floor spaces.

In conclusion one perhaps ought to call attention to the fact that the article more generally associated with Kashmir than any other, that is the Kashmir shawl, is no longer manufactured in the Valley, nor has it been for a number of years. These beautiful fabrics are now a "drug on the market" and can be had for a song. Yet one can see from the designs shown that it is a pity that it is becoming a lost art.

ARTICLES OF PAPIER MÂCHÉ, SILVER, BRASS AND WOOD EXQUISITELY DESIGNED

The two papier mâché vases are done in the beautiful colors of the Kashmir shawl; the perfume sprinkler and bowl beneath it are of silver and show almost incredible skill for detail and beauty of design; the box to the left is used for burning incense; and the other vase is of brass and is both hammered and engraved.

XII

SOCIAL LIFE

*"And the nightingale's hymn from the Isle of Chenars
Is broken by laughs and light echoes of feet
From the cool, shining walks where the young people meet"*
—*Lalla Rookh.*

VERY much could be said about the social life in the Valley, but the chief factors are the British Resident and the Maharaja. I put the Resident first simply because I do not feel qualified to say very much about the native social life. The Residency was, at least during our stay in Kashmir, the chief center of social life among the English-speaking residents and visitors, although it so happened at this time that the Maharaja, as will be seen from the chapter devoted to him, entered far more into this society than he had hitherto, on account of the numerous festivities that celebrated the marriage of his handsome and engaging heir—his nephew.

The Stuart-Frasers—the Resident, his wife and charming family—were, as a Scottish gentleman said, the very soul of hospitality, and as will be seen in the chapter devoted to the Residency, this lovely spot was the gathering place of pretty much all the English-speaking residents, both permanent and official. Every week there were events of some kind and some weeks there were several; all were charming and delightful not only because of the cordial hospitality, but also on account of the fascinating informal atmosphere that prevailed. There was a certain amount of modified state and formality, but it was so graciously blended with perfect ease and charm of manner that it had all the winsomeness of a sort of glorified English country house life. Indeed, at times it was hard to realize that you were thousands of miles from England, so entirely was this true. But there were other factors in this social life beside these, as all the members of the Resident's official family, as well as the English officials associated with

THE VALE OF KASHMIR

the Maharaja's developments of his realm, took a delightful and prominent part. They also gave dinners, receptions and dances so often that there was no time for tedium or "to kill." Moreover, these are remembered by the writer as among the most delightful souvenirs of life in the Valley. Then, too, the Chaplain's home was a frequent gathering place of all who cared to come for teas, badminton parties and receptions. Another prominent factor was the family of the head of the Church Mission School, and many a delightful day is associated with them, not only at the school and their home, but also at the picturesque al fresco teas beside the lake, where the guests were asked to witness the regattas and the swimming and diving contests, as well as other water sports.

The Neve brothers likewise filled an important place in this social life, not only at the hospital, where visitors were numerous and cordially welcomed, but at the picturesque home beside the river of Arthur Neve and his wife. No experience in the Valley is likely to be remembered longer than a visit to the lovely spot where the lepers live, and afternoon tea was served in the boats under the shadow of those splendid chenar trees that provide delicious shade in some of the harbor nooks along the lake. The beauty of these was enhanced by the wonderful coloring at sunset, as one rowed down the lake to the Dhal gate.

Nor do these events by any means exhaust the list of delightful social gatherings, for pretty much everybody did something and as the cottages and houseboats were numerous there was hardly a day that did not have some form of entertainment and some days had many, sometimes in the lovely gardens of the cottages, at others in the houseboats on the river or on the roof of the boats under the awnings, or again on the river bank under the shade of the trees or the protecting shelter of a marquee. It was a never-failing pleasure to simply row up and down the river and watch the pretty pictures of the social life as we passed along.

A GARDEN PARTY AT THE RESIDENCY

The Honorable Resident conferring a Kaiser-i-Hind medal of the first class upon the Reverend C. E. Tyndale-Biscoe, under the shadow of the British flag. The Maharaja will be seen in the center background, applauding, with the members of his own and the Resident's staff.

THE VALE OF KASHMIR

Then, too, the Club was the daily gathering place for nearly everyone. There were certain hours in the morning and afternoon when you were sure to meet a large number of your friends in or about the Club. Tennis, riding, golf and polo had their place as purely social factors, for the number of charmingly dressed girls and women who were onlookers far outnumbered the players. There was no lack of social life and at times it seemed as though there was more than one could take advantage of. While it is certainly true that one who comes with letters enters into this social life far more quickly and pleasantly than one who does not, yet so real is this hospitality that the wish of all seems to be to promote the happiness of as many as possible.

Naturally, a large proportion of the temporary residents are officers and their families who have come from their different posts for a little refreshment and change, but as many of them have seen service in various parts of the world, there is a cosmopolitan atmosphere that is very agreeable after the insularity and provincialism met in some quarters. Of course this life would not be quite complete without a slight measure of gossip and mild scandal, but this is, as a rule, of so comparatively harmless a character that it gives what some consider a very welcome zest to the day's experiences.

One rather surprising feature is to find that native princes and their wives are to some extent a part of the social life here. One of them was almost constantly seen on the polo fields, the golf links, in the Gulmarg Club, and even in private houses. Yet more surprising still was the unusual popularity of a certain Begum, who with her husband had traveled extensively and who was here a great favorite among the cottagers, with some of whom she had tea, or to whom she gave tea almost daily. Naturally as this particular lady was in purdah, being a Mohammedan, the male contingent were supposed to see little if anything of her features, but as this purdah sometimes consisted merely of the protection afforded by a small sunshade drawn down over her head when she was on her walks through the woods, walkers and riders had occasional accidental glimpses of her face. Nor was this purdah assumed because of prejudices, for she had dressed as Europeans do when on her travels, but was now worn simply as a recognition of what was expected of her by her own people when in her own country. It will perhaps be seen from all this that the social life in the Valley may claim variety as well as charm.

XIII

THE RESIDENCY

"Visions by day and feasts by night"
—*Lalla Rookh.*

THE grounds of the Residency stretch along the river bank at a point where it is especially attractive and in the section where the Club and many official residences are to be found. Several of the latter are embowered in flowers in a way that is wonderfully beautiful and entirely indescribable. From the shady walk that skirts the bank of the river for several miles one gets a good view of the river façade of the Residency and the impression is of a large but charming home, rather than a vast and pretentious palace, and this impression is intensified when you have passed through the portals to the grounds and stand on the lovely lawn under the shade of those splendid trees and beside the beautifully flowering plants, bushes and trees, with the other vine-covered façade just in front of you. Nor is this impression disturbed when you enter the hall or go about through the delightful rooms. It is merely just such an interior as the exterior would lead you to expect, and precisely the sort of atmosphere that you would find in any of the lovely homes of England. Indeed at the first dinner given us at the Residency we several times forgot that we were not in England and found ourselves speaking just as though we were there. While it is true it is not England, yet somehow this atmosphere makes you feel at times as though this must be a fascinating English home with its beautiful park and glorious vistas and its delightful expression of hospitality. Again, it is indeed hard to realize that England is thousands of miles away, and when you are attending a ball or reception in these delightful rooms it is almost impossible to believe that you are two hundred miles from the nearest railroad station.

THE VALE OF KASHMIR

As already intimated, the hospitality of the Residency is worthy of the house and setting. It is true that this might not be the same, or at least not quite the same, if there were not a charming host and hostess with an equally charming family. At this time there were two daughters, who were called by their friends and admirers "the rosebuds." It all seemed just as it should be, harmonious and complete, and from early in April till late in October the Residency breathed hospitality, whether here or in Gulmarg. We had only been in the Valley a few days when we received an invitation to a lawn fête, and after that it was a succession of garden parties, tennis parties, luncheons, dinners, dances, tableaux and concerts.

Here, too, one met not only all of the Resident's official family and their wives and children, but also all of the distinguished visitors and officials who were passing through Kashmir. It was here that all important functions were held, save of course such as were more fitting in the Maharaja's palace. Possibly the most delightful features, if one may choose any special features among so many that are equally delightful, were the garden parties, and as one moved about among the noble shade trees and saw the British flag flying from the flag-staff in the distant vista, the landscape garden effects represented so fascinating a blending of things English and things Kashmiri that not infrequently people had a feeling of being in the grounds of Windsor Castle, instead of those of the Residency in Kashmir.

These garden parties, too, were chosen as happy moments for the conferring of medals and honors in behalf of the King or the Maharaja. For instance, at a garden party held on the twenty-third of May, 1912, the Honorable Resident in Kashmir presented a Kaisar-i-Hind medal of the first class to the Reverend C. E. Tyndale-Biscoe. In doing this the Honorable Mr. Stuart-Fraser said:

"It is a privilege which I value highly to be charged by His Excellency, the Viceroy, with the presentation to the

Here is shown the Seventh Bridge that crosses the Jhelum at the outskirts of Srinagar. In the distance is seen the Hill of the Fort that stands as sentinel to the city.

The garden façade of the British Residency, which for a large portion of the year fairly glows with floral beauty and reminds the traveler of a beautiful English country home.

THE VALE OF KASHMIR

Rev. Mr. Tyndale-Biscoe, here in the presence of His Highness the Maharaja and his many other Indian and European admirers, of the Kaisar-i-Hind medal of the first class, which was conferred upon him at the time of the Delhi Coronation Durbar. There is so much that might be said about Mr. Biscoe that I find it not easy to choose my words, and to cut this function as short as he—the most modest of men—would, I feel, like. His work is generally known to all who know Kashmir. For over twenty years Mr. Biscoe, as principal of the Church Missionary Society schools, has devoted his life, and—if he will let me add—his money to the task of teaching the youth of Kashmir and training their moral and physical qualities. A man of dominating personality by the application of public school and commonsense methods, by his insight into human nature, and above all by his own life and courageous example, he has—after overcoming difficulties that would have defeated any one not gifted with his enthusiasm and happy sense of humor—succeeded in establishing a position for his schools unique in this or any other State. While his pupils are well taught and hold their own with any in the examinations, the feature which distinguishes Mr. Biscoe's from all other schools that I, at least, have seen in India is his marvelous success in building up the character as well as the bodies of his boys.

"An old Cambridge Blue, he has taught the Kashmiri pundit to row and to rejoice in rowing; himself a notable swimmer, he has produced a school of swimmers, and I don't know of any other set of boys who could perform as they do the feat of swimming across the Dhal and the Wular Lakes. Mr. Biscoe asks no one to do what he cannot do himself and if you will visit his schools you will see the boys of all ages practicing the art of self-defense, which he has taught them, with boxing gloves and single-sticks. But more remarkable is what Mr. Biscoe has done for the characters of his pupils. We hear much in these days about the need for moral teaching and the problem is the most difficult one that faces the edu-

THE VALE OF KASHMIR

cationist. The solution is not a matter of text-books but of example, and the difficulty would disappear if there were more men like Mr. Biscoe. Practical morality is his principle, and long before the Boy Scout movement—than which there has seldom I think appeared one so full of hope for the Anglo-Saxon race—had taught thousands of boys in England and the Colonies the ambition of doing some one a good turn if possible, every day, Mr. Biscoe had been teaching his boys here in Srinagar by example as well as by precept the dignity of service. His boys save lives from drowning, they assist at putting out fires in the city, they help the weak and decrepit in the streets, they take out convalescents from the hospitals for outings on the river and lake, and they are imbibing from their master his righteous intolerance of cruelty to animals.

"Ladies and gentlemen, these achievements sound wonderful, but since I have come to Kashmir I have seen for myself how they are really taking place. And there is reason to believe that Mr. Biscoe's influence on the character of his pupils is one that persists beyond their school days and goes with them into life and service. Kashmir owes an incalculable debt to Mr. Biscoe. But the gain of Kashmir has been the loss of England, for I use the language of no conventional compliment in expressing my belief that he is one of those rare-born leaders of boys and men who would have been a tower of strength to any of our most famous public schools at home. The motto of his schools is: In all things be men. Mr. Tyndale-Biscoe is a man, and he is one of whom we are all proud. Long may he be here to continue his great work in our midst."

A LIVING WELCOME TO THE MAHARAJA

While many think that the present rulers of India only play at royalty, that their thrones are but pleasing conceits and their scepters empty baubles allowed to them by an indulgent overlord, the Maharaja of Kashmir is a free agent in all material things and the allegiance of the populace to him is very real.

XIV
THE MAHARAJA

*"Th' imperial Selim held a feast
In his magnificent Shalimar"*
—*Lalla Rookh.*

HIS Highness Major-General Sir Pratap Singh, G. C. S. I., Maharaja of Jammu and Kashmir, is considered by many to be one of the most interesting and picturesque Oriental rulers associated with the British Dominions, and while he is a man well past middle life, he is well preserved and active, and seems much younger than he is. His dominions of Jammu and Kashmir cover an extensive area and comprise, as has already been indicated, some of the most beautiful and strikingly picturesque portions of the world. The population is not large, probably less than four million, and the ruler inherited his domains from his father, who received them from their founder, Gulab Singh, his grandfather.

Owing to the variety of climatic conditions, he has practically three distinct homes, one in Jammu, where he lives during the winter; one in Srinagar, where he has a very fine palace and extensive grounds and makes his home during spring and autumn; and the third is his mountain home in Gulmarg, where he is in residence during July and August. His popularity among all classes is indicated by the warmth and cordiality of the welcome he receives each year when he returns to his palace in Srinagar. As will be seen by one of the pictures, so enthusiastic were his subjects on one occasion that the river was spanned by ropes so tied together that the acrobatic members of Mr. Tyndale-Biscoe's school were able to arrange themselves in such a way that the positions of their bodies spelled the word "Welcome."

Another of the pictures shows the Maharaja arriving in his royal boat, attended by a retinue of officers and servants, and a vast horde of admirers in smaller boats. On these occasions all the buildings lining the banks of the river, and all

THE VALE OF KASHMIR

the boats upon the river are gaily decorated with flags, bunting and lanterns, and on one or two nights, at least, the vicinity of his palace is made exceedingly brilliant by the superb display of fireworks.

While this welcome is extended to him every year, it was of an especially interesting nature at the time of our visit because of the added feature of his nephew's recent marriage, and the extensive and delightful hospitalities in connection with this event, one of the first being the state dinner, to which the invitation was as follows:

> His Highness Major-General Sir Pratap Singh, G.C.S.I.
> Maharaja of Jammu and Kashmir
> requests the pleasure of
> Rev. and Mrs. Ward Denys'
> company at Dinner
> on Tuesday, the 3rd of June, at 7.40 p. m.   R. S. V. P. to Assistant Resident

This dinner would have been considered a brilliant occasion in almost any part of the world, and it had the usual speeches and toasts of welcome. Preceding it was a reception, at which all were presented to the Maharaja or paid him their respects. It was a very interesting mingling of European costumes with Oriental color, the heir apparent being clad in superb garments and adorned with gorgeous jewels of almost incalculable value. In order that it may be seen how almost lavish was this monarch's hospitality, the following menu is given:

MENU	WINES	
Hors d'oeuvres Variées	SHERRY	La Torre
	VIN BLANC	Graves
Consommé Fausse Tortue	HOCK	Hockheimer
Potage Crême d'Asperges		
	BURGUNDY	Beaune
Truite Bouilli See Hollandaise		Yalumba
Cailles à la Bourdelaise	CLARET	St. Julien
Cotelettes en chaudfroid aux Champignons farcies	CHAMPAGNE	Bollinger 1904
Selle de Mouton rôti	PORT	Camroux & Co.
Salade de Saison		White & Tawney
Canetons aux Petits Pois	LIQUERS	Kummel
		Creme de Menthe
Pyramide de Macarons au Chocolat		Benedictine
Péches Melba		Grand Marnier
Jambon Grillée au Madére	COGNAC	Justerini and Brooks
Desert		

PRINCE HARI SINGH, THE HEIR APPARENT TO THE THRONE

The Prince is the nephew of the Maharaja and is the successor to the throne of Jammu and Kashmir. He is a young man of striking personality, a sportsman proficient in polo, golf and cricket, and is held in high esteem.

THE VALE OF KASHMIR

Throughout the dinner the native band played the following pieces of music:

PROGRAMME OF MUSIC

1.	March	"Scipio"	*Handel*
2.	Overture	"Light Cavalry"	*Suppe*
3.	Morceau	"St. Malo"	*Kiefert*
4.	Suite	"Russe"	*Kanz*
5.	Duet	"Under the Moon"	*Lauder*
6.	Galop	"Wally"	*Phillips*

This dinner was followed by a series of festivities and entertainments of all sorts that lasted until the 14th of June, and concluded with another dinner given in honor of the wedding of Raja Humar Hari Singh Sahib. This differed little from the other save that on this occasion the Maharaja himself read a somewhat extensive speech in English, beginning with: "I feel highly honored by your cordial acceptance of my invitation to grace this festive occasion," and ending with these words: "I therefore ask you, ladies and gentlemen, to be good enough to drink to the health of my dear nephew, Hari Singh, may he live long and be happy and prosperous."

Among the various parties, receptions and dinners, perhaps none was more charming than the garden party given at the Nishat Bagh, one of the most beautiful of all the gardens belonging to the Maharaja. This garden owes its beauty not only to its wonderful landscape features of trees, shrubs, flowers, pools, cascades, temples and pagodas, but also to the extensive view that it commands of the Dhal Lake and the superb panorama of mountain peaks, rising above twenty thousand feet in height and all clad with a beautiful white mantle throughout the year.

At this particular garden party practically all of the British residents of the Valley were present, as well as all of the Maharaja's officers of state and the chief citizens. At the dinners there were probably between two and three hundred guests, but at this garden party they must have counted into the thousands. There seemed to be an almost endless proces-

THE VALE OF KASHMIR

sion of vehicles on the way to the garden, which is several miles distant from Srinagar, and a perfect flotilla of boats, as it is possible to approach by both land and water.

Another event of especial interest was the cricket match, in which the Maharaja himself took part. He is a keen lover of sport of all kinds, excepting sport that means the taking of life, in which he never indulges. His love of cricket, for instance, is so great that, in spite of his years, he never fails to take part in a certain number of matches, and he is as keen as the youngest member present in the matter of making as large a score as possible. Nor is this interest discouraged by his British friends, who see to it that his score is always a satisfactory one to himself. Of course he does not attempt to run —that is done by another for him—but he does bat and sometimes surprisingly well. Naturally when he makes a particularly good hit the native enthusiasm is almost wild in its demonstration of delight, but it is well sustained by all the members of the British community who are present. At this and all similar occasions there is a tent, or oftentimes three or four tents, where refreshments of all sorts are served on a very liberal scale. Nothing is stinted as to quantity or quality, and the very best that can be had is invariably provided, even in the matter of liquors and cigars.

Another event in which the Maharaja felt a very keen interest was the polo match, in which his nephew, Hari Singh, took part as captain of the native team. This nephew, by-the-bye, is a good all-round sport and a splendid specimen of manly vigor and beauty. Moreover, he seems to have the true spirit of a real sport, for he is as able to accept defeat as he is success. He is also a very good golfer and tennis player, but the Maharaja, his uncle, does not attempt either of these games.

The following invitation, from which it will be seen that even the children were included in this series of wedding festivities, will indicate how thoughtful the Maharaja was of persons of all ages.

The chief palace of His Highness, The Maharaja, at Srinagar, whose impressive façade rises sheer from the waters of the Jhelum.

Most any member of the family is pressed into this service. Here the daughter is assisting, while the young son trots along to see that the job is well done.

HIS HIGHNESS THE MAHARAJA WITH THE NATIVE CRICKET TEAMS AT GULMARG

Keen interest is taken in the cricket matches that are held at frequent intervals and they are always affairs of social interest. Among the spectators here shown are the British Resident and his party.

THE VALE OF KASHMIR

Rajkumar Hari Singh Sahib's Wedding Festivities
His Highness The Maharaja of Kashmir
AT HOME
on Friday, 13th June, at Rajkumar, Hari Singh's Shergarhi House,
at 5.30 P. M.

Children's Party

During July and August, as already stated, the court moves to Gulmarg, and when I say the "court" I mean the Maharaja and his entourage, as well as the British Resident, and the officials associated with him in the administration of British interests in Kashmir. There at an elevation of eight thousand five hundred feet, the Maharaja has a series of cottages where he lives during these two months. The days are far too short for the social and other activities that take place; for it is a continuous series of golf, tennis, dances, dinners, afternoon receptions and balls. In all of these the Maharaja takes a deep interest and some of them he attends in person. During our stay in Srinagar he was present at the garden parties given by the British Resident on a number of occasions, and on one of them, when a sale was being held in behalf of a local charity, the Maharaja was one of the most generous purchasers. Indeed, he was so generous that when he happened to win a valuable article in a lottery, he instantly returned it and it was sold at auction for a very large sum.

It will be seen that there is no effort being made in this chapter to give a biography or history of the Maharaja, but merely some slight idea of his personality, in the hope that it may be shown why he is so popular and so highly esteemed.

XV
THE CLUB

*"If woman can make the worst wilderness dear,
Think, think what a heaven she must make of Cashmere"*
—*Lalla Rookh.*

PROBABLY nothing holds a more important place in the social life of all who come to the Valley than the Club. It is, in a sense, a center of life at all seasons of the year, though during the spring and autumn when the number of visitors is at its maximum it plays a more important rôle than at any other time.

It is very fortunate in its situation as its grounds join those of the Residency, being separated only by a narrow lane. Its outlook on the river is probably the most delightful one upon the bank, which at this point is perhaps higher than almost anywhere else, and the space has been increased by a sort of balcony that has been built out over the river itself. This balcony is so large as to form a kind of square in front of the Club. The side adjoining the river is a continuous series of benches, and from these one not only has an extensive view of some miles up and down the river, but also of the beautiful country on the opposite bank and the mountain wall beyond. This square, as well as all the verandas of the Club, presents a very charming and animated picture for an hour or two before luncheon, and again from afternoon tea on until dinner time, as these are the hours when nearly everybody tries to look in at least for a few minutes.

The Club house itself is very well adapted to the purpose, having reading rooms, card rooms, refreshment rooms, a library and large assembly room. Here one can find all of the leading English and Indian papers and magazines, and by English I mean some of those printed in America as well. The library itself is unusually well selected, especially with reference to matters of local interest in Kashmir and its surroundings.

The Srinagar Club, always the scene of life and gaiety, has an ideal setting in the shade of a magnificent chenar grove on the mirrored waters of the Jhelum with the Takht as a background.

The entrance to Gulmarg is lined with native bazaars. Gulmarg is the official summer home of the Maharaja and the British Resident. The Gulmarg Club and cottages are seen in the distance.

THE VALE OF KASHMIR

The tennis-courts are just in the rear of the Club and at certain seasons are almost too popular, so great is the number wishing to play, and the tennis tournaments are certain of a large and interested gallery. From time to time entertainments are given in the assembly room, and now and then occur illustrated lectures by distinguished travelers or mountain climbers. While this Club is devoted chiefly to English and Europeans, one sometimes sees native princes, though rarely, if ever, any of the local native residents.

The golf links are also connected with this Club, although they are some distance away. But the tennis players, golf players, polo players and cricket players, all find their way to the Club at the conclusion of their games and the assemblage is very frequently a gay and merry one. The requisites for admission are simple and the fees are very light.

There is one feature of the Club that makes it quite unusual and that is the kitchen garden, in which various fresh vegetables are raised and sold to members of the Club at practically cost prices. The importance of this is appreciated by those who live there and realize how necessary it is to exercise the greatest care in all sanitary matters, for the Kashmiri, like all Orientals, are inclined to be very careless and indifferent about such things, with the result that enteric diseases are more or less common and sometimes very severe.

Owing to the situation of the Club upon the bank of the river, which has a delightful walk several miles in length that runs in front of some of the more interesting residences and important shops and, for the most part, is deliciously shaded by the huge and beautiful chenar trees, it is easily possible for one who wishes to see friends to simply wait until they pass by, for nearly all of the residents in the city are pretty sure to go up and down at least twice a day on their way to the post office or the shops, or to make calls.

It will be seen, therefore, that this Club not only has very attractive but also very practical advantages, not the least of which is its accessibility from the river by boat and from the

THE VALE OF KASHMIR

land by carriages, horses and on foot. As it is adjacent to the Residency the members can always learn the latest telegraphic news from all parts of the world by simply crossing the path and reading the bulletins that are posted in the main portal to the Residency grounds.

BRITISH POLO TEAM IN THE VALLEY OF GULMARG

Many of these mounts would compare favorably with the best ponies to be found in any part of the world and the players are very skilled. In fact there are two excellent teams in Kashmir, the one of high caste natives headed by the Heir Apparent and the other of British officers stationed in various parts of India.

XVI
SPORTS

"And waked to moonlight and to play"
—*Lalla Rookh.*

SPORTS naturally fill a very important place in a community that is in a sense very largely of a vacation character, for during the season the majority of the temporary residents are there simply for their vacations. They consist largely of civil and military officials with their wives and families, pretty nearly all of whom are not only accustomed to the various forms of sport, but as a rule are extremely fond of them. Among these, as already intimated in other chapters, tennis, golf, polo, cricket, badminton, croquet, sailing and riding fill an important place.

TENNIS

The tennis-courts are in almost constant use at the Club as well as at the Residency, which has several beautiful courts that are open to the use of the guests of the Resident, and the numerous private courts are all equally busy, but the interest in this sport centers chiefly around the tournament season when prizes are awarded; and some fine records have been made.

GOLF

Golf in India is played pretty nearly everywhere. There are few communities, even the smaller ones, where there is not some provision made for this sport, although as a rule it is not as good as that in Srinagar or Gulmarg. And possibly there is no one sport that fills so large a place among the active and vigorous members of the community as golf. For instance, in Gulmarg there are two eighteen-hole courses, each of which would compare well with the best courses in any part of the world, and both of these are crowded to their full

THE VALE OF KASHMIR

capacity ofttimes even in bad weather, throughout the months of July and August.

So general and so intense is this devotion to golf that people who are somewhat indifferent about it almost dread to go to Gulmarg, where golf is not only the principal subject of conversation, but results, as a certain officer said, in the air being so full of golf balls that it is almost dangerous to go about unless you are a player yourself. This is literally true, for one who is riding or walking in the vicinity of these links has to exercise the greatest care, in spite of which some rather disagreeable accidents occur from time to time.

POLO

While all this is true with regard to golf it is doubtful if it arouses as much interest as the polo games, at which the crowds, not only of Europeans, but of natives, are enormous and extremely enthusiastic. This is in part due to the fact that the heir to the throne, Hari Singh, is devoted to this sport and is the captain of the native team, all of whom are considered "crack" players. So the enthusiasm and interest on the part of the Kashmiri is if anything greater than that of the English residents, who are inclined to take things as a matter of course and not to be very demonstrative.

These polo players are mostly British officers and come from various parts of India, bringing their strings of ponies with them, and many of these would compare well with the very best ponies to be found in any part of the world. The result of all this is that there are sometimes very brilliant games that would be of interest anywhere and a credit in any country. The provision made for these polo matches, too, is an excellent one, for about half a mile back from the river there is a large common about a mile in length and nearly a half mile in width that is devoted to polo, cricket and other sports, and as there are roads and trees surrounding this, it is easily accessible from all sides.

YOUNG KASHMIR AT PLAY

Children's games seem to be universal in their nature. For example, here in far-off Kashmir the children are playing the well-known game of hop-scotch. The mud-daubed, thatched house, from which peers the patriarch of the family, is typical of the average dwelling house of Kashmir.

THE VALE OF KASHMIR

CRICKET

The mere fact that the Maharaja is a cricketer gives a zest to this sport that it otherwise would not possess, at least among the natives. It is, however, a very popular one among the officers and residents, and some of the teams make a most creditable showing. Naturally the largest attendance is drawn together when it is known the Maharaja himself is going to take part. This attendance is composed largely of ladies, and it would be hard to conceive a more charming picture than these attractive English women present in their dainty afternoon costumes.

BADMINTON

Badminton has the distinction of being a sport in which all ages take part, and I have seen ladies and gentlemen who were well toward eighty playing this game with great interest and gusto. As it may not be as familiar to American readers as the other sports, possibly a line or two with regard to it may be of interest. In a word, something like a small tennis racket or battledore is used as a bat or racket, and something resembling the shuttlecock takes the place of a ball. A tennis net is stretched at an elevation of seven or eight feet, and the game consists of batting this shuttlecock from side to side, with three people on each side instead of two as in the case of tennis.

The reason why even elderly people like this game is that it can be played very quietly if all of the participants are of about the same age, whereas when the contestants are younger it becomes quite as exciting and vigorous as a well-fought game of tennis. It happens, too, to be the one game that is of a distinctly social character, and during the season hardly a day passes that somebody doesn't give a badminton party, which takes the place of an afternoon tea, the badminton being provided for those who care to play (and most of the guests do if only for a few moments at a time), while the refreshment provision at tables and in the shade is continuous and the opportunity for a diverting interchange of gossip never ceases.

CROQUET

Croquet has perhaps more devotees in the Valley that it would have at any of the average summer resorts in other parts of the world, but for the most part it is restricted to those who do not care for a very active form of sport, or who, for some reason, are unable to indulge in anything of that sort. The game, however, is played on courts that are so well constructed and laid out that it is something like a game of billiards as an evidence of skill. It is therefore this element of interest that gives it an exceptional place in the esteem of a certain portion of the community.

SAILING

By sailing I do not mean sailing in a sailboat, but being rowed in a rowboat or going about in a motorboat, as there are a number of these on the river; and of all the pleasures that the Valley affords there is none perhaps more delightful than this, because in this way you not only call on your friends who live in the houseboats that line the banks of the river for many miles, but you can also do your shopping. As will be seen later on, this is the most agreeable way of seeing the banks of the river and the life along those banks. It is, however, entirely apart from these features, delightful in itself, for nothing could be more beautiful than a row on the river under the awnings that are provided with all the rowboats, at the hour when the sun is beginning to fall behind the mountain wall in the distance. This is due partly to the fact that the twilight and sunset effects seem to linger longer here than almost anywhere else. When the sun goes behind this mountain wall, its light continues for a very long time reflected from the sky, and at this hour, too, the temperature is most agreeable. Consequently one is pretty sure to find a large number of one's friends on the river at this time of day.

THE VALE OF KASHMIR

RIDING

Riding is as general here as it is in the home country, for, as will be understood, nearly all of the officers and their wives have their own saddle-horses that they bring with them, and the resident community is equally well equipped, so that the temporary visitors who come without horses have merely to turn to the Maharaja's stables and he, hospitable man, has a large stud, some of which are very good mounts and all of which are rented by the month for a relatively nominal charge. It will be seen from statements elsewhere that it is not an extravagant indulgence, nor is there any sport that offers more varied features of interest than this, because of the fine roads, delightful paths and gloriously beautiful country.

THE REGATTAS

In conclusion one should not forget the regattas that are held each year by the members of Mr. Tyndale-Biscoe's school. While these are spoken of in the chapter devoted to the school itself, they constitute so important a place in the interests of the community that they should be mentioned here as well. Their success naturally is due to the competent training of the head of the school, who has introduced as far as possible English ways and English ideals, and the feats of running, swimming and diving are surprising to even experienced athletes.

XVII

THE VALLEY AND MOUNTAINS

> "And Day, with his banner of radiance unfurled,
> Shines in through the mountainous portal that opes,
> Sublime, from that Valley of bliss to the world"
> —*Lalla Rookh*.

SOMETHING has already been said about both the Valley and mountains, but it would be quite impossible to do full justice to either, so rich is this wonderful Valley in features of beauty and interest, and so impressive and varied is the mountain wall that surrounds it. There are several points of view from which one can gain distinct impressions of different parts of the Valley, and possibly none offers so great a treat as that from the Takht-i-Suleiman, which, as stated elsewhere, rises almost from the center of the city in the form of a splendid pyramid to a height of a thousand feet above the river. From the top of this the whole Valley stretches out before you, the view of the Dhal Lake being especially fine. The flashing windings of the river, seen through the trees, are visible for many miles in each direction, while off in the distance toward Baramulla lies the Wular Lake.

This, too, is one of the most delightful points from which to view the blossoms, and probably no richer feast of glorious color has ever been provided on the face of this earth than is presented by the Valley when all the different fruit trees are in bloom. Many even go so far as to say that they think the cherry blossoms of Srinagar are more beautiful, because of their massing of effects, than those of Japan. With this, however, I cannot agree, though they are wonderfully beautiful, and this display of glorious color begins with the first blossom and does not end until all have finished their bloom, which covers a very long period of time.

Then, too, the hills themselves undergo a process of transformation, for what during the winter has become brown and arid as the spring-time advances begins to glow with vivid

WHERE EIGHT THOUSAND FEET ABOVE THE SEA IS A LOWLAND

Here nestled in a setting of the world's mightiest mountains, is a little valley, the Lidar, 8,000 feet above sea level, and 3,000 feet above the main Valley of Kashmir. It is watered by a silver ribbon of a stream fed from the eternal snow-crowned giants who rear their heads to the dizzy height of nearly 28,000 feet above the sea.

tones. This is so striking that it is almost difficult to realize that it is the same hill now that was so bleak and barren a short time ago.

From this point also one gets a very excellent view of the various royal gardens that surround the extensive shores of the Dhal Lake, while just across the city rises the hill upon which the fort is built. This also offers a fine panorama, and, while it is not so extensive as that from the Takht, it gives more of the details in the nearby effects.

Still another superb point of view is the plateau of Martund, to which allusion will be made later on. And still another, and perhaps the most striking of all, is from what is called the "Outer Road" that circles the precipice surrounding Gulmarg, from which almost the entire Valley can be seen as well as some of the higher mountain peaks, which appear here to better advantage than almost anywhere else in the Valley.

But while we have been speaking of the Valley of Kashmir as though it were one, it is as a matter of fact many. This one large valley, with its two huge lakes and rivers, is surrounded by a whole family of valleys, each of which offers to the lover of nature a wonderful treat in the way of striking and picturesque landscape effects. So numerous are these valleys that, so to speak, empty into or open out from the main valley, that volumes could be written about them. Each of them has as its advocates and to them the visitors go during the hot months of July and August according to their tastes and inclinations. They are all for the most part from one to three thousand feet higher than the Valley of Kashmir itself, and by this I mean the valley and the level where Srinagar is built.

XVIII

PLACES OF WORSHIP

"When the shrines through the foliage are gleaming half shown,
And each hallows the hour by some rites of its own"
—*Lalla Rookh*.

OF these there are many in the Valley of Kashmir, and especially in the city of Srinagar—Hindu temples and Mohammedan mosques and Christian churches. The Hindu temples are for the most part the splendid ruins that are to be seen in different parts of the Valley, and to which a chapter is devoted elsewhere. There are, however, a few of these that are still in use. There is an interesting shrine near, or practically a part of the Maharaja's palace, where there are some handsomely illuminated missals and Hindu sacred books.

Of the mosques there are naturally many more, as three-fourths of the population is Mohammedan, although as elsewhere stated the Maharaja is himself a Hindu. Among these the Shah Hamadan Mosque, which stands on the right bank, is probably one of the finest specimens of a building of this sort. This is entirely of wood, the slabs of the sides being laid in such a way that they resemble brick. The carving in the windows is of a very pleasing character, and the roof, which is lofty, is surmounted by an open spire with a gilded ball—a very characteristic treatment in this part of the world. The best view to be had of this mosque is from the opposite bank, where it is seen with the hill of the fort rising in the background.

One of the most popular Mohammedan shrines lies at the foot of the hill of the fort and is called Makhdum Shahs Ziarat. It is to this shrine that large numbers of people rush in case of sickness, as there is a popular superstition that a visit will result in a cure.

Of the churches there are two that are doing a very useful work in addition to that which is being done among the natives at the Church Mission School and the Mission Hospital. One

The English Church, with its vine-covered Rectory, which seems to typify by its peaceful surroundings religious freedom, in marked contrast to the temple-crowned Takht symbolizing autocratic power.

Both the Hindus and the followers of Mohammed are continuously making pilgrimages to some sacred shrine or other. This is a portion of the procession on its way to the sacred Cave of Amarnath.

THE VALE OF KASHMIR

of them is the little Roman Catholic Chapel and the other the beautifully situated and very attractive English Church. This, with its picturesque Rectory, in the midst of a wealth of flowers, trees and shrubs, is easily one of the most charming features in the city and very fittingly fills an important place in the religious and social life of the English-speaking population. The services are well attended, and the congregation was very fortunate in having, at the time of our visit, an unusually good preacher, as well as an efficient pastor, in Mr. Fellows. While he did everything in his power to make the services interesting, attractive and helpful and was very faithful in caring for the needs of the resident community and in visiting all who were good enough to give him their addresses, he was ably assisted by his wife, who made the Rectory a sort of parochial social center, giving frequent afternoon teas and badminton parties and receptions, to which all who were interested were invited to come and were made acquainted with one another.

While this chapel, or church, is devoted chiefly to the resident English and the visitors, a great deal is done directly and indirectly in behalf of the natives. Although no services are held there in the native language, yet the influence of this church is felt in various parts of the city because of the way in which those associated with the church come in contact with the native community. For instance, the treasurer, or rather the secretary, of the church was also the owner of the carpet factory and had in his employ several hundred men, and his daily intimate dealings with his employees and their families brought the influence of the church directly into the life of his workers, at least in so far as the practical application of the principles of Christianity to daily life are concerned. It is very comforting to see what a tone this indirect influence has given to all who were brought under it.

XIX
ANCIENT TEMPLES

"The mighty ruins where they stood,
Upon the mount's high, rocky verge"
—*Lalla Rookh.*

THIS subject is so unfamiliar the writer does not hesitate to say that before his own visit to the Valley he had no idea that there were any ruins of exceptional interest in that remote and beautiful part of the world.

Nor has he happened to meet any archæologist who had, although he has met many in his search for information. Even in Kashmir itself the few who were interested knew comparatively little about the ruins they had seen and admired. There were, however, a few books in the Club library in Srinagar that told something about them, but personal friends who had photographed or sketched them knew little more than the pictures showed.

But if there was a poverty of information in these sources, it was more than made up by the extravagant exuberance of the native imagination, which provides a host of fabulous tales. Some of these have been translated and published in English, and one small book shown the writer at Martund claimed that these particular ruins were several thousand years old.

This paucity of information is unfortunate, as any one can see from the photographs that the ruins are of great interest, and a few words in regard to some of the more important may help to show that they are worthy of far more thorough investigation than they have yet received.

Perhaps sometime an expert may be sent to study them so that more light may be thrown upon them, but until something of this sort is done we must be content with what we have, and what the pictures show us.

That they are worthy of this interest the writer is fully convinced, because they easily hold their own when compared

The smaller temple at Avantipur, not far from the river's brink, where the excavations have already brought to light beautiful skeletons of stone buildings.

The ruined temple of Bhaniyar as seen in its glorious emerald setting. This is the first temple to greet you and the last to say good-bye.

THE VALE OF KASHMIR

to the great and well-known monuments and ruins of Europe, Asia, and Africa, most of which he has visited many times at leisure.

There are certain things and places like the ruins of Rome, Greece, and Egypt, the Taj Mahal, the view of the Himalayan giants from Darjeeling, the Yosemite, the Grand Canyon, Niagara Falls, and others that stand out prominently in one's memory, and in reviewing them the visit to Martund, at sunrise takes a prominent place. But the mental pictures one forms of them, from the description in the guide-books and elsewhere, are far from definite, nor do they give the faintest promise of the delightful and interesting memories they leave behind.

So little were we prepared for what was in store for us, that when we passed Bhaniyar, on our way into Srinagar, we hardly more than glanced at the ruins, and yet they offer features of exceptional interest, but we made ample amends for this omission some months later, when we were coming out of the Valley. This it was easy to do as the temples lie quite near the road, and are less than two miles from the village of Naushera.

Here we have one of the earliest examples of a temple that retains its original enclosure. This is in the form of a cloistered quadrangle about one hundred and fifty feet square, with a shrine and cella of unusually large and noble proportions, being thirteen and a half feet square in the interior with walls that are nearly seven feet thick.

Unfortunately the more delicate carvings and ornamentations have been nearly obliterated by time, but the walls, which are pierced by a series of pedimented and trefoil arches, are in a wonderful state of preservation, and the impression made by the use of the trefoil, here and elsewhere in Kashmir, upon one accustomed to its use and significance in Christian decoration, is peculiar and indescribable as it is so startlingly suggestive of the deep underlying unities that seem to pervade all religious thought and symbolism.

THE VALE OF KASHMIR

But if the temples of Bhaniyar did not hold our attention long when we were on our way in, the Takht-i-Suleiman did, and that too from the moment we caught sight of it in the Valley, nor did this prominent feature in the landscape ever fail to delight us although we lived under its shadow for many months. This striking mountain—it is about six thousand two hundred and fifty feet above the level of the sea—rises like a splendid pyramid from the city of Srinagar to the height of over a thousand feet, and is crowned by one of the most picturesque and impressive temples in the entire Valley. The moment we saw it, in spite of our fatigue due to our two hundred miles ride, we were refreshed at once, nor did the prospect ever fail to produce a sensation of delight.

This temple is one of the oldest in Kashmir and, although it has been rebuilt, perhaps more than once, it is, as the picture indicates, a very remarkable structure, on account of the stone work.

There is a good path from the hospital in the city all the way to the top, and it is a favorite walk, not only on account of the temple, but because of the superb view it commands of the Dhal Lake and the entire Valley.

Of the temple itself much might be said, but let it suffice to say that it is constructed in horizontal courses without cement, and that it has a small dark circular inner shrine.

About three miles north of the Takht, and in the centre of what was once the old city of Srinagar, though very few traces of it now remain, is the extremely interesting temple of Pandrathan. It stands in the midst of what was once a small pond—now dry—and is about eighteen feet square with a projecting portico on either side. It is richly decorated, and the domed roof is worthy of careful study, for the sculpture is so purely classical in design as to suggest a Greek or Roman origin, although it is said to have been erected between 913 and 921 A. D. by Meru, Prime Minister to King Partha.

Still further up the river, and not far from the bank, lie the extensive temples of Avantipur which until quite recently

THE VALE OF KASHMIR

had been buried, but the excavations have already brought to light many remains of great interest, for it was here at his capital city that the famous King Avanti Varmma founded two temples and dedicated them to Mahadeva some time between 858 and 883 A. D. At the present time a good idea of their size, and the quality of the work, can be formed from the gateways and the colonnades of the smaller of the two, and one cannot help noting their resemblance in style to those at Martund, but perhaps the greatest interest will be felt in the elaborate carvings that enrich the semi-detached pillars of the arched recesses, which are of a very variegated and pleasing character.

But of all the temple ruins seen in Kashmir those at Martund are easily the most impressive, not only on account of their extent, but because of the great beauty of their wonderful situation.

The sail up the Jhelum to Islamabad, and the ride from there up to the lofty plateau, that commands vast stretches of the Valley with its silvery, serpentine river, is an experience that can never be forgotten, especially if it is made in time to see the sun rise and stream through the eastern portal to bathe the rich interior with golden splendor.

As the smiling native custodian greets you, he hands you a copy of the native history and description of the ruins. In this the claim is made that the first structure was erected some four thousand years ago while the English and other archæologists place it between 360 and 383 A. D., but, however this may be, these are easily the most imposing, as well as the most beautiful, of all the ruins in Kashmir, and this is the only temple that has a choir and nave in addition to the cella or sanctuary. This nave is about eighteen feet square, and the entire length of the structure is sixty-three feet. For the most part it is quite plain, but the two adjoining compartments have richly decorated panels and elaborately sculptured niches. It is difficult to determine the exact height, as the

THE VALE OF KASHMIR

roof has been removed and lies in masses on the ground, but it is believed to have been about seventy-five feet.

A wide flight of steps approaches the western entrance, which is surmounted by a superb trefoiled arch, with chapels on either side, one of which is connected with the nave. The other side has equally impressive arches with closed doorways beneath. The quadrangle, which is pillared, is about two hundred and twenty by one hundred and forty-two feet and is decorated with the most elaborate carvings in Kashmir. There are eighty-four fluted columns with beautiful capitals, a number considered sacred by the Hindus, being a multiple of the signs of the zodiac and the days of the week.

This work is ascribed to the famous King Lalitaditya, who reigned between 699 and 735 A. D. But probably that which will impress the average lover of the beautiful most will be the almost startling suggestiveness of Greek influence at its very best period, though how this influence came to this remote part of the world at a time when it was almost inaccessible, no records declare, but however it came it is a thousand pities that these beautiful gems of architecture should have been so terribly mutilated by fanatical Moslems, and yet even in their present state so impressive is their beauty that one admirer said, "that they were easily the most interesting feature among a host of interesting features that the Vale of Kashmir affords to delight the traveler."

There are many other ruins of interest in the Valley of Kashmir, but the foregoing will amply serve the writer's purpose in calling attention to them.

NOTE. This Chapter is a reprint of an article by Dr. Denys on the Ancient Temples of Kashmir, which appeared in Vol. 1, No. 2, of "Art and Archaeology," and is used by their permission.

The Temple of Martund, showing the trefoil arch, the carving, and a portion of the cloister that surrounds the quadrangle.

The Temple of Pandrathan, seen at a time when the tank surrounding it was dry, although the small boat used to visit the interior can be seen at the left.

XX

HOSPITALS

> "Who could have thought, that there, e'en there,
> Amid those scenes so still and fair,
> The Demon of the Plague hath cast
> From his hot wing a deadlier blast"
> —*Lalla Rookh.*

OF these there are several, and while the State Hospital is a large and well-equipped building with a competent corps of physicians and nurses, I shall confine what I have to say chiefly to three: the Cottage, or Visitors' Hospital; the Mission Hospital; and the Leper Hospital.

The first of these is, as its name implies, a large cottage beautifully embowered in shade and flowers and of easy access to the resident portion of the city, in so far as it concerns Europeans and visitors, for whom this cottage is especially intended, as the hotels, cottages and houseboats are not very satisfactory places to care for an invalid who is seriously ill. Here there is a resident physician, and any of the physicians in the Valley are at liberty to bring patients and to care for them. No one can realize how great a boon a provision of this kind is until he has had personal experience, and then it cannot be too highly praised, for here not only does the patient have expert medical treatment, but the most careful trained nursing. Every provision is made for the treatment of disease and the comfort of the patients that the limited area of the structure will permit, and it is highly probable that a great many lives have been saved simply because it has been possible to take them to a place of this sort where they could receive just the care required.

This work is supported by subscriptions given by the visitors themselves, fees paid by the patients, collections that are occasionally taken up in the churches, and the entertainments that are given in its behalf. The subscribers are entitled to care and attendance at reduced rates, which is sometimes a very great boon to people whose incomes are limited and who are unfortunate enough to have serious illness away from home.

The interest taken in this work is very great on the part of all and by no one more than the Resident and his family—at least that was the case when we were there at the time the Hon. Stuart-Fraser was Resident. So great was this interest that he gave the Residency Garden on one occasion for a tableau concert in behalf of this hospital, at which very beautiful and very creditable renderings were given.

The Mission Hospital fills also a very large and important place among the natives, not only of Srinagar but the whole Valley of Kashmir, and it would be hard to find anywhere in the world two more devoted men than the Neve brothers, the elder of whom, Arthur, has been connected with this work for many years. In order that my readers may have some idea of the conditions these hospital workers have to contend with, I wish to quote the following:

"Any real sanitation requires the intelligent co-operation of the people, who as a whole seem as opposed to sanitary reform as to religious changes; they seem as wedded to their primitive dirty habits as to their superstitions. The condition of all the narrow back-streets in Srinagar is unspeakably filthy, and even the wealthy make no attempts to keep their own courtyards clean. In a town like Islamabad people bathe, wash clothes and drink water at the same small tank, though it would be perfectly easy to reserve the spring for drinking and to make washing places a few yards further down."

Naturally conditions of this kind result in an exceptional amount of disease, and to the care of this the workers in the Mission Hospital continually devote themselves.

The buildings are very delightfully situated on the crest of a small hill at the edge of the city, and just at the foot of the Takht there is a group of buildings as well adapted to the needs of the situation as the means at the disposal of the mission authorities would permit, and a visit to this hospital

Dr. Arthur Neve and his assistants caring for the sick in a remote country village. The traveling dispensary is seen at the right.

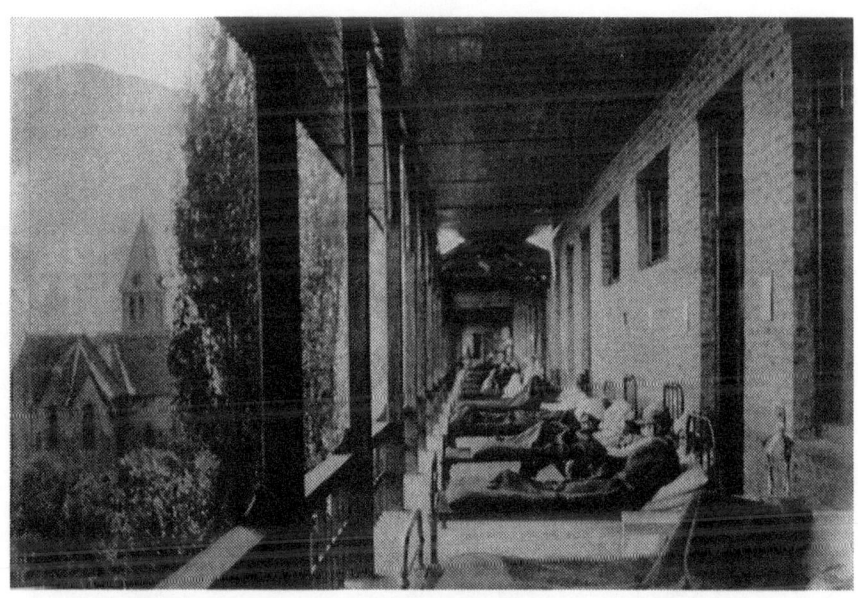

Convalescents in an out-ward of the Mission Hospital. This Hospital is a marvel of equipment, efficiency, cleanliness and good cheer.

THE VALE OF KASHMIR

on the part of one who has seen some of the best hospitals in the world—that is as far as their equipment is concerned—is a revelation and a surprise, for while everything is simple there seems to be a provision for almost everything that is required in a hospital that is considered up to date in European countries or in America at the present time. The electrical apparatus, while not extensive, is adequate in so far as it goes and fills a very important place, although possibly that which is more astonishing to the average visitor is the X-ray apparatus, which had very kindly been given to the hospital by friends and had been successfully installed a short time before our visit. So necessary was this particular apparatus that it was in almost daily use and a number of obscure diseases had been made clear, and fractures and heart difficulties diagnosed. All the wards were well fitted up and very clean and carefully served by well-trained native attendants. Then there is an out-of-door provision of several balconies with long rows of cots, and there are also wards for private cases where one can be entirely by himself and see friends when the condition warrants it.

Services are held every day and are attended by as many of the patients as are able to walk, and the doctors told me that it was very gratifying to find that a better feeling toward Christianity was gradually becoming established and that they did attend these services now very much more freely than they had in the past and that the feeling on the part of their families and friends was far more sympathetic. All of which was attributed in a large measure to the great benefit that the hospital had conferred upon the diseased and afflicted members of the Kashmir community.

Possibly it may be of interest to my readers to know how a visit to this hospital impressed the Viceroy, who made the following remarks in the Visitors' Book:

"It has given me the greatest possible pleasure to visit this Hospital. Its organization and management are thoroughly up to date, and the amount of work that is done is immense; but the feature that has struck me most is the spirit of life and energy that marks its whole tone. I congratulate Dr. Neve on his work and the State of Kashmir upon its possession of so beneficent an institution."

HARDINGE OF PENSHURST.

Also in another communication:

"I feel I have a very lasting and most pleasing recollection of my visit to the Mission Hospital in Srinagar. I had heard so much of this Institution and of the work of the Doctors Neve that I now wish to thank them for their kindness in showing me a hospital managed with so much skill, care and devotion."

WINIFRED HARDINGE OF PENSHURST.

Nor is the work of this hospital by any means confined to the buildings or the city, for these brothers go away on what might be called medical missionary tours from time to time, and during one of these tours of three weeks they treated about eight hundred patients in ten different places, five of which had never been visited before. They said that the officials met them and were very friendly and helpful. On one occasion they were very much surprised by the fact that several who had previously been at the hospital, and some of whom had been cured, brought little gifts of fruits and eggs as an evidence that they had appreciated the kindnesses they had received.

In a community such as is to be found in the Valley of Kashmir, eye troubles are very frequent and in the course of a single year eleven hundred and seventy operations were performed for eye diseases alone. One hundred and thirty-six of these were for cataract, and one hundred and twenty-two of this number who had been previously quite blind were restored to sight. This is a remarkable record in view of the fact that while it is comparatively easy to perform the operation to cure the disease, it is almost impossible to persuade the patients and their families to do their part in caring for

A NATIVE HUT IN THE VILLAGE OF ATCHIBAL

Whatever may be said of the Kashmiris' disregard for Occidental standards of sanitation, full credit must be given to them for their practice of frequent bathing. These falls mark one of the most beautiful spots on the road to Phalgram and are popular with the bathers.

THE VALE OF KASHMIR

themselves after the treatment. The success of this work is further shown by the fact that in a total of five thousand operations in one year, both major and minor, only one-half of one per cent. were unsuccessful.

In conclusion a word must be said in behalf of the very noble work that is done at what is called the State Leper Hospital by these doctors and Mrs. Neve. I rowed one afternoon through the fascinating waters and lakes and bays and dells that make up the shore of the Dhal Lake, and after entering an exceptionally lovely little bay, climbed to the site of the Leper Hospital buildings. These are numerous and devoted to various purposes. For instance, one of them is the kitchen—a very important building because it requires the greatest care to see that the food in its preparation is not contaminated. For the most part, however, these buildings are little detached cottages, sometimes having three or four rooms, in each of which a leper, or a leper and his wife and children reside. Entire freedom is permitted here and the healthy members of the leper's family are associated with the diseased without restraint and just as they would be in their own home. Every effort, however, is made on the part of the authorities, who have as their chief Dr. Arthur Neve, to train the people to observe the necessary sanitary precautions. There is no law in the matter on the part of the State, and if patients come they come voluntarily. Lepers are permitted, if they choose to do so, to live in their own homes, so that the care for, and treatment of, this disease is not as systematic, thorough and effective as it would otherwise be, and the absence of any rigid rules in the hospital itself makes the care of the patients one of great difficulty and patience on the part of the doctors and nurses, and yet, in spite of this, no small measure of success has been obtained. During one year, for instance, one hundred and three new lepers were admitted and quite a percentage showed very marked improvement. A visit to this hospital naturally brings with it many very depressing experiences, for some of these patients are in a repulsive and almost loathsome condition. And yet the devotion of the wife to the husband, when the husband is in an advanced stage of the disease and the wife perfectly healthy, is touching and beautiful. But it is startling to see a little child playing with a father in such a state as this. It was, however, very comforting to go from room to room and find them for the most part cheerful, happy and contented. There was little suffering and no complaining at all. One poor man, who was without family, had embraced Christianity and, being bedridden, was very grateful to any who might call on him to read to him, and among the number was a little boy, who had been taught by one of the Christian teachers how to read. This little boy used to entertain the old man, and the old man himself, in return, taught the little fellow the meaning of Christianity, and he became so impressed with these stories of the life of Christ that he wanted to be baptized. His parents, who were lepers (although the little boy himself was apparently perfectly healthy), objected, as they were Hindus and he, they felt, would become an outcast, although they themselves were practically paupers and being supported by the State and the generosity of charitable friends. At last, however, they were so persuaded by the beautiful character of the old man and the great devotion of the little boy that they permitted him to be baptized, and at the same time virtually gave their son to this old gentleman in order that, as he was to be a Christian, he might have a Christian father.

XXI

SCHOOLS

> "A prophet of the Truth whose mission draws
> Its rights from heaven"
> —*Lalla Rookh*.

IN this chapter it is my wish to speak of the vital and in many respects trying work that is being done by and under the inspiration of one of the finest and most sensible heroes I have ever met.

So modestly and so quietly has this remarkable work been done by Mr. Tyndale-Biscoe that it was not until I called on the wife of the British Resident that I even heard of either the man or his work.

Mrs. Stuart-Fraser had been speaking of the neighbors in the Valley, and the tone of her voice as well as the expression of her face when she referred to Mr. Tyndale-Biscoe made me feel that he was held in high esteem by all. We were greatly pleased, therefore, a few days later to receive an invitation to lunch at the school that is under his care.

This we accepted with pleasure, and we were agreeably surprised to learn that the varied and delicious food that was served in one of the large halls, for there were more than thirty guests present, had been prepared by people connected with the school. All around us as we ate were evidences of a profound knowledge of human nature, especially human nature that needs unconscious objective training.

Conspicuous among these was the school motto and crest. It is in the form of a shield with the motto, "In all things be men," just inside the border, above which is a pair of crossed paddles with heart-shaped blades. Of this the following is said in one of the school booklets: "We mean by a man, one who is both strong and kind." The crest also bears out this idea. The paddle stands for hard work or strength, the heart-shaped paddle for kindness. The paddles are crossed, which stands for self-sacrifice, and reminds men of Him who taught us self-sacrifice and all that His Cross means to the world."

This it will be seen at once tells its own story, and makes its own impression. Moreover, this symbol of sanity, balance, and uplift is a key to the wonderful success and far-reaching usefulness of the work done in the school.

Another evidence of thoroughness is seen in the charts of the boys' character form sheets on which minute and discriminating data are recorded in regard to each boy in the school.

This is divided into three parts: mind, body, and soul, and the latter is again subdivided into three parts, (1) conduct toward masters, boys, school, and city; (2) manners, deportment, absence of tricks, and self-control; (3) discipline, cleanliness of body and clothes, attendance, and punctuality.

It is, of course, impossible to mention more than a few of the items in this chart, but its far-reaching value and influence are appreciated in proportion to the extent and variety of one's experience in dealing with natives in this part of the world.

After luncheon we visited all the rooms of the school and found that western ideals had been introduced wherever they had any place in such a setting, but always with due deference to the local atmosphere.

And one is struck by the contrast to what is found in the native schools in other parts of the East; for instance, in many the scholars and teachers squat on the floor and study aloud as they sway their bodies from side to side for hours, accompanied at times by a disgusting, sucking sound like that made by some men when they drink hot soup.

All this was the case here, and lying was the rule when Mr. Tyndale-Biscoe came, but now one is impressed by the quiet seriousness of the teachers and scholars, and the orderliness of the rooms, while lying is the exception instead of the rule.

THE CHURCH MISSION SCHOOL WELCOMING HIS HIGHNESS

This unique Mission School of the Church of England is a potent factor in the upbuilding of Kashmir. It is held in high esteem by both the people and the ruler. Here each year a royal welcome is accorded the Maharaja on his return to his palace at Srinagar.

THE VALE OF KASHMIR

We then went into the large quadrangle which was entirely empty, but the moment the gong sounded all the scholars of certain classes appeared from various parts of the buildings and came to the ground in a variety of ways as quickly as the members of a fire engine squad would assemble for a fire.

We then had athletics of all sorts, including some pretty fair boxing, and, strange as it may seem, this boxing is one of the most practical and valuable assets of the school and community, for it has enabled the teachers and scholars to protect many an innocent victim from robbery and murderous assault.

While these exercises were going on the school band was playing, and playing well. At the close of all I had the pleasure of making a short address to the fifteen hundred scholars, and hearing their cordial hurrahs.

On another day we had tea beside the lake and saw some fine rowing, paddling, swimming, and diving that would have done credit to any western school. All of this seems simple and natural enough to us in the West, but before any of it could be brought to pass some of the most hardened fanatical religious and superstitious prejudices had to be overcome, and the history of the school is rich in amusing and interesting incidents that have marked its progress.

On still another day I went to talk to the teachers, about eighty in number, in English, which they speak and understand remarkably well. They sat in a semi-circle in front of me under the shade of one of the beautiful chenar trees, and when I asked them what they would like me to talk about, they said, "America or New York," as though they were one and the same thing, for big and important as we may seem in the West, comparatively little is known about us in that remote Valley.

Among other things I spoke of the height of the buildings, and these elevations seemed so incredible to them that they took frequent advantage of my request to ask questions. They

THE VALE OF KASHMIR

wanted to know how such high buildings could be made to stand, and after I had explained their construction they put many very pertinent queries as to light, air, and appearance.

But I have now said enough to introduce this school to my readers, and the pictures will do the rest. My only regret is that it is impossible to give some of the illuminating and interesting stories told me by the principal, who, if he had remained in England, would undoubtedly have been one of the most potent and valuable educational influences in that country, but who, nevertheless, seems very happy "going about doing good" just where he is in the Vale of Kashmir.

KILLING THE DEMONS OF WULAR LAKE.

The narrow flat boats of the natives capsize easily in the squalls that frequent this lake. The superstition is that demons infest these waters and that it is useless to attempt to escape, but the Mission School is overcoming this foolish belief by demonstrating that even the youngsters can swim the six miles of the lake unharmed.

XXII

TRAVELING IN A HOUSEBOAT

> "Beneath them, waves of crystal move
> In silent swell—heaven glows above"
> —*Lalla Rookh.*

THE two most popular river trips that are made in houseboats are those to Ganderbal and Islamabad, one being down the river and the other up, and in this way one is able to enjoy all the life and beauty of the river scenery while traveling in his own house, with all the servants, the kitchen boat and rowboats. It is important, however, to make these trips during the more favorable seasons, either in June or September, preferably the former, as all the verdure is fresh and the flowers in abundant bloom during that month.

So one beautiful June morning soon after sunrise we made our start for Ganderbal. As this was our first experience in traveling in a houseboat, we were all on the upper deck under the awning in our easy chairs to take in the features of the departure. All our own regular servants were in traveling costume, which means that they had stripped off everything that the law would permit, so that if anyone fell overboard he would be clad as lightly as possible. And this was an accident (if it may be so termed) that happened not infrequently. At first it is a bit alarming, but after it has happened a number of times you get accustomed to it and hardly notice the yells and struggles and efforts to save the apparently drowning man.

The stakes to which the ropes and chains were attached were pulled up, for the boat was fastened to the bank by a heavy iron chain at either end with ropes between, as we had been tied up to the bank for a very long time. This was especially necessary in the case of the *Diana*, as owing to her exceptional size much greater care was required in all her arrangements. In spite of the heat we had a large number of

THE VALE OF KASHMIR

natives, presumably friends of the servants, to see us off, and conspicuous among them were a policeman and a letter-carrier. Just why they were there we did not understand, as we had never seen either of them before, having gone to the postoffice ourselves, or sent there for all our letters, none of them ever having been delivered. But they made themselves so very conspicuous and officious that I asked my head boatman what it meant, and he told me that they had appeared in order that I might know who they were and possibly be inclined to give them a tip. When I asked him what service they had rendered, he said he didn't know of any, but that this was a habit of these men and that whenever a boat left the landing or the bank they would at least give the travelers an opportunity to recognize their existence. I said: "How much of an insult do you think would be satisfactory to them?" Sultana, my steward, who had charge of all the affairs of the boat, overhearing this, said he thought a very small one, and asked if I would be willing to give each of them a couple of annas, or about four cents each. As this didn't seem like a very serious and dangerous precedent I consented, with the understanding that they should be very modest in future in any demands that they might be inclined to make.

I also noticed servants from the houses of our various friends, who had brought letters to us and flowers, fruits, etc., from their employers. They were all in their smartest attire in honor of the occasion, and while they said nothing, their manner indicated that they expected something. They, too, were easily satisfied, and when the stakes were pulled up and the chains and ropes taken aboard, which was done in the midst of an immense amount of yelling and shouting, the boat swung slowly out into the current, which at this point and at that season was pretty swift, and it required the services of a dozen trackers, who served as rowers, or punters, to keep the huge Diana in the proper course. All of these efforts seemed to give great delight to the crowd of men and women and children who had assembled upon the bank. One

WAYFARERS ON THE ROAD FROM SRINAGAR TO BARAMULLA
It is thirty miles between these two cities and the broad way is lined on each side by symmetrically beautiful poplars, that afford a vista that could scarce be equalled anywhere else in the world.

THE VALE OF KASHMIR

would think, perhaps, that this was a very rare and exceptional event, but it isn't, for boats are coming and going continually, and yet the natives find these incidents so much more interesting than their duties, or work, that they avail themselves of the very slightest excuse to become onlookers.

The chief boatman, who was the owner of our kitchen boat and who with his family lived in the kitchen boat, at least in one end of it (though how they all occupied this six by six strip of deck when there were two husbands, two wives, two small boys and one baby, we never knew), took entire charge of the expedition, although he took his orders from Sultana, who received them from myself. This meant that the head boatman had something like twenty people under his direction. They were divided up along the side of the boat, each one having a certain portion of the space on the little passageway which is about fourteen inches wide and runs along the outside of the boat throughout its entire length. They also served as rowers and sometimes they punted and sometimes they did something like rowing. They would all go toward the bow to the limit of their spaces and then thrust their poles in where the water was not too deep and would push the boat along, walking as they went to the other end of their beats. There was also a man with an oar at the front of the boat and one in the rear to assist in guiding, acting as helmsmen.

Altogether it was a very interesting and novel experience. It was not, however, without some slight accidents, such as bumping into other boats and stirring up the servants and occupants in them, some of whom were still enjoying their early morning slumbers and were very much enraged at being disturbed. This naturally resulted in some rather noisy verbal interchanges between the servants of the different boats, a great deal of shaking of fists and sticks, and occasionally the shying of some vegetable at one another. These little pleasantries, however, were soon over and we were in the midst of the stream on our way down the river, and from the start all the way through the city under each of these seven bridges the experience was one of unalloyed delight, so much so that we had our breakfast served on the deck instead of going below to the dining-room as we had been accustomed to do, since we did not wish to lose a single moment of this interesting panorama which we were seeing for the first time from such an elevation. Hitherto our sails up and down the river had been in the small rowboat, but now we looked down upon all the smaller craft and were on a level with the tops of the bank in many places so that we had a fine view of all the features of the river life and scenery.

This feature itself, if one did not go beyond the limits of the city, would amply repay for all the expense and trouble. We had not realized how much better it was possible to see things from this elevation than from the level of the water in a rowboat. We had, too, an excellent opportunity to study the curious and fantastical architecture of this motley conglomeration of buildings, and got a very much better idea of the Maharaja's fine palace, as well as the adjacent palaces, buildings and grounds, than we had ever had before. The experience, too, was enriched by passing the Maharaja's state barge, as well as that of the Resident, each of which was filled with gaily costumed rowers and an exceedingly picturesque cockswain. Both of these are handsome boats and the oarsmen row in almost mathematical unison.

When we had passed the limits of the city the banks were more even and lower, so that we could readily see over them, and it was interesting, too, to note the line of the road from Srinagar to Baramulla on the one side, which was seen across a perfectly level meadow some distance away, and was indicated by the long rows of shade trees that lined it on either side. All the way along there were little houses and occasionally hamlets. At this point we began to make remarkably good speed, as some of the trackers went ashore and pulled, while the others punted and rowed.

As stated in other chapters, the river bank through the city is lined with houseboats and all sorts of crafts, the lower

THE VALE OF KASHMIR

portions being devoted chiefly to native houseboats, and this continued more or less of the distance to our first halting place, where we tied up for the night. We had, therefore, after leaving the city several hours of delightful and restful experience, during which we could look over the banks and the long stretches of country clear to the distant mountain wall on either hand.

The only incident of exceptional interest was the passing of a mad woman, who was groveling on the bank. One of our boatmen went ashore to see what the difficulty was and found a beautiful young woman, not more than nineteen years of age, who had been cast off by her husband and had lost her little child. The result of this husband's brutal treatment, coupled with the loss of the infant, had so unsettled her reason that she went about sleeping in the fields or elsewhere, and from time to time pleading and crying for her husband to come back, or calling for her child. The poor soul had frequently little or nothing to eat—indeed, when we first saw her she was grabbing up and putting in her mouth some refuse that was on the towpath. It was quite touching to see how kind the boatmen were to this unfortunate, but the women were apparently afraid to go near her, as she was an object of almost superstitious veneration on account of her being, as they termed it, "possessed of the spirit."

Near sunset the lights and color effects were very beautiful, as we pulled up to the shore to tie up for the night at Shadipur, where there is a large grove of very beautiful chenar trees. It is a particularly nice place for houseboats to moor in the cold water of the Sind River, which presents a striking contrast to that of the Jhelum, the latter being dirty and muddy and more or less filled with all sorts of rubbish, while the water of the Sind is as clear as crystal and almost as cold as ice—so clear that you readily see the bottom almost anywhere, and so cold that it doesn't require any ice. Here, with the boat in the shade of some of these splendid old trees, we had our dinner on the bank, the table, dishes, etc., having been placed there in order that we might have this agreeable experience. And so polite and considerate were the natives who lived in the village a short distance away that none of them came near to annoy or disturb us, or even pay their respects until after this meal was over, when some came to extend a welcome to friends among the servants, and to ask who we were and other questions prompted by curiosity and interest. We had also a charming walk in the twilight, so the day was a full one as well as very agreeable.

Another view of the Lidar Valley, at a point above Phalgram. The wild grandeur of this scenery beggars description and must be seen to be appreciated.

The Lidar River is a turbulent stream that sweeps down from the mountains through the Lidar Valley. It is especially beautiful here at Gulmarg as it flows over rapids and its waters are tossed into a white foaming spray.

XXIII

GANDERBAL

> "And, suddenly, a tuneful breeze,
> As full of small, rich harmonies
> As ever wind, that o'er the tents
> Of Azab blew, was full of scents."
> —*Lalla Rookh.*

THE following morning we were up, at least the boatmen were, at daybreak, making preparations to go up the Sind, indeed the boat was detached from the bank and the trackers started on their way. But before we had gone more than a hundred yards, the boat was fast against the bank. After a long time it was pulled away and then we made another short distance, with a similar experience. This was repeated for the third time when Sultana came to me and said that the head boatman was afraid it would be impossible for him to get up the river, as the current was so swift, the river was so narrow, and our boat so very large and cumbersome.

This was exceedingly disappointing information, as one of our chief pleasures had been the anticipation of just this sail up the Sind River. A conference was held with Sultana, the head boatman, and the captain of the coolies, which resulted in their saying that they would try to go on if I insisted on it, but that it would probably take several days to get as far as Ganderbal, and, as the time ordinarily required was only a few hours, we didn't look forward to this snail-like progress with any pleasure. However, they concluded to make one further effort, and all went fairly well until we came to a sharp turn in the river, and here the great length of the boat made it impossible for us to go around, and we were fast at each end and in the middle. This was so discouraging that we had another conference and the result of that was that we concluded to accept the suggestion of the head boatman to have the kitchen boat cleaned up and one of the compartments

THE VALE OF KASHMIR

(for they are open on the sides, having merely a sort of an awning that falls down to protect them from the sun and weather) prepared for our use so that we could be pulled up the river in that. These arrangements were carried out in a very short time and we were very much pleased at the way in which they had spread the rugs on the floor of this compartment and arranged our easy chairs and books and other articles that we would wish on the way up the river. After this our progress was very rapid, for this was a real boat, pointed at each end and intended for sailing purposes, and not like the houseboat, intended chiefly for dwelling purposes.

Indeed, we went so smoothly and rapidly that we reached Ganderbal just after tiffin, which we had had served on the bank in the shade of some delightful chenar trees. Our friends who had been staying in Ganderbal were just taking their after-tiffin siesta, from which we awakened them by our arrival.

The river at this point broadens out somewhat, but is fairly choked by the number of houseboats, some of which are pretty large, but most of which are of the kind called dungah boats, which are a sort of boat and houseboat with pointed ends for sailing in shallow water and around crooked turns. This spot, as will be inferred from the large number who were there, is a very favorite one at this season, and in fact many remain there all summer, there being few if any mosquitoes and the air is cooled by the water, which comes fresh from the melting snow and ice of the mountains, which are only a short distance away. There was formerly a stone bridge across the river at this point, but it has been destroyed and now there are merely the picturesque remains of three of the arches.

Most of the people had brought their tents with them and were camping in the shade of the trees on the shores, or back on the plain, but as it had been rather dry, there having been very little rainfall for some time, the grass was brown and withered and everything looked rather arid and dusty, so that we were a little disappointed in Ganderbal, of which we had

SHISHA NAG GLACIER MET EN ROUTE TO THE CAVE OF AMARNATH

The word Himalaya is derived from two Indian words, meaning "Halls of Snow," and the lucky traveler who journeys to the Sacred Cave of Amarnath realizes the significance of this name, for he must negotiate this mighty glacier and is surrounded on every side and walks through glistening corridors mantled in snow and ice.

heard such glowing descriptions. But the people there seemed to have a very good time—there were picnics and excursions, afternoon teas, badminton parties and dances almost daily, not to mention fishing and hunting, the former being especially good owing to the coldness of the water, and never have we eaten more delicious fish than those that were caught and cooked while we were there.

We had so many friends, or so many invitations from different friends to afternoon tea that our family was divided and went in six different directions, and when we reassembled, about five o'clock, we started on our return journey down the river. So swift was the current that we reached the Diana, which had been taken back to her former mooring, in good time for dinner, and there we passed our second night, which was not as quiet as the first had been, owing to the visit of some strange dogs from an adjacent community. These so-called pie dogs, or mongrels, as a rule are rather mangy-looking and great cowards, but they serve as scavengers and to some extent as protectors. But when visiting dogs come to a community their welcome is likely to be of so warm a character that if they escape with their lives they are fortunate, and our impression was that the visitors and the residents must have been pretty evenly balanced, because the row went on at intervals nearly all night.

Our return up the river the following day was very much slower, not only owing to the fact that we were going against the current with a very large boat, but we were unfortunate enough to have a heavy wind-storm which made it almost impossible to move the boat at all. Indeed we were tied up at times for an hour or more waiting for a lull in the storm before we could proceed. And at last when we reached the city, instead of attempting to go through the river as we had in coming down, we were pulled into one of the canals (for the country in and about the city is intersected by a perfect network of these canals, some of which cut off the sharp turns in the river and make it possible to go from point to point

THE VALE OF KASHMIR

very much more rapidly), and while we avoided the wind, the canal was so narrow and there were so many other boats in it, some of which were apparently trying to do what we were, that our progress was very slow, and the rows were almost incessant for it was well-nigh impossible to avoid collision with so many boats going and coming—or attempting to go and come—in this limited space. All of which meant that it was about half-past ten when we succeeded in finding a mooring on the bank in the upper part of the city, not where we had been before, for our own mooring was taken almost before we left it, as it was considered so desirable. We had been there such a long time, and the rule is that the last comer has to take what he can find and be content until somebody else moves out. Sometimes it is very funny to see three or four boats all trying to get the same place at the same time.

PLOWING IN THE VALLEY

Modern agricultural implements are practically unknown here, and the husbandman turns up the fertile soil with only the assistance of this primitive plow drawn by oxen or in many cases with a sharpened root drawn by a couple of men and held down by a third.

XXIV

ISLAMABAD

"Shooting around their jasper fount
Her little garden mosque to see"
—*Lalla Rookh.*

ON another glorious June day we made an equally early start for Islamabad, and this was, in a different way, quite as interesting as the trip to Ganderbal, but it requires considerably more time as the distance is much greater. From the standpoint of river scenery this is distinctly more interesting than the trip to Ganderbal, for the river is crossed by bridges at times, and the groves of chenar and other trees are in some places wonderfully beautiful. There are also a number of villages, as will be seen.

At the outset our departure was punctuated at very frequent intervals by greetings from our friends who were tied up in their boats along the bank, and at some of these boats we paused for a little visit. Owing to the boat being so large our progress against the current was naturally very slow and on one or two occasions we were tied up on sandbanks, to our great disgust, for some time. But we succeeded in reaching a point near Pampur for the night, and nowhere—not even in Egypt or Venice—had we had more gorgeous sunset effects than we had here. I wish it were possible to convey some idea of the great beauty of these light and color effects on the magnificent evergreen trees and the picturesque groups of native houses that line the shore.

It was so late that we did not attempt to go ashore, deferring that until our return voyage. The next morning we were off at daybreak, and passed Avantipur, where we paused only long enough to make a few purchases, tying up for the night at a beautiful spot on the bank of the river not far from one of the exceedingly picturesque bridges.

The following morning we again made a very early start and stopped for the night at a picturesque village called

THE VALE OF KASHMIR

Sangram. The next day was our last before reaching Islamabad and one of the most interesting as well, because we paused for afternoon tea at what is perhaps the finest chenar grove in the Valley of Kashmir, near a place called Bijbehara, where we also met some of our Srinagar friends who were camping before going on to Pahlgam. Later we continued on to the landing in Islamabad, where there were almost numberless boats and many interesting events all the time we were there day and night.

We were fortunate in securing a good place at which to tie up, Sultana having bribed a native boat to go away and let us have it. Islamabad is a very interesting point, not only because of the trees, the native life, the beauty of the situation, and the river and land scenery, but because of the large number of visitors who are there and the number of horses and donkeys required to make the various excursions.

Our arrangements for the following day were completed before we retired and at six o'clock the next morning our cavalcade of equestrians started for Martund. The road for the most part, until we reached the point where we began to climb the mountain, was very dusty and the ascent to the plateau pretty steep. It was a ride of about six miles, and one of our party who was not fond of horseback was carried up in what is called a "dandy," which somewhat resembles an old-fashioned coffin on poles.

Our ride was enlivened by a shower of rain, which fortunately was over before we reached the temples. It would be hard to find a more impressive site than that upon which these temples are built, and the air is delicious at this elevation and the view very beautiful, for the Valley stretches out before you for many miles and the river at that distance looks like a silver serpent winding among the trees. Of the temples themselves a description will be found elsewhere and I will merely mention here that the visit ranks in interest with the most memorable ones that we have had in any part of the world, even the visit to the pyramids in Egypt.

THE VALE OF KASHMIR

On our return across this plateau we were very much interested in the farmers and their primitive mode of tilling the soil, which sometimes was done by a sharpened root drawn by a couple of men and held by a third. We passed a number of flocks of goats and sheep, but not many cows.

The surroundings of Islamabad, because of the beautiful gardens, are of exceptional interest, and the royal fish-ponds, with the sacred fish, are visited not only by thousands of the natives but great numbers of tourists. We were back in time not only to visit these gardens and many of the streets and bazaars, but for a late tiffin, and able to get away from this maddening babble of sounds at three o'clock in the afternoon. It was particularly delightful to lounge in our easy chairs on our upper deck and enjoy the rare beauty of the scenery on the way down the river to Bijbehara, where we were to camp for the night. Our friends had gone and we had this vast beautifully laid out grove entirely to ourselves—not even the natives were about. The town, which is just across the river, was far enough away to be very picturesque without disturbing us.

Our dinner was served under the shade of one of these splendid trees, and after we had visited the various features of interest, including the remains of a fountain and some carved work, we paused to view the ruins of the temple, in the midst of a cluster of trees and shrubs, and near which were encamped the so-called holy men. These men are clad as a rule simply as nature made them, with possibly a very abbreviated loin cloth, and their bodies seemed to have been smeared with oil and then sprinkled with ashes. As many of them have tawny-colored hair (whether it is produced by art or is natural I do not know), they present a very striking appearance, especially as some of them are quite young and handsome while others have long black beards, and still others gray or white hair and beards. They live on what is given them and have no covering, as a rule, save that of the sky, nor any couch save that of the ground. Beside the bank were a number of houseboats belonging to people who had gone on with their tents and camps for a tour through the mountains or a stay at Pahlgam.

The following day we had a stretch of very steep bank, with precipitous steps from the water to the top, and in fact there were two or three flights of these steps at intervals. Although it was about five o'clock in the morning, there were men at one, women at another, and men and women together at a third, while way off on the hillside were the scantily clad shepherds surrounded by their flocks of sheep or herds of goats charmingly silhouetted against the golden sky.

About noon we reached Avantipur again and went ashore to visit the various temples, a brief description of which will be found elsewhere. Here, or soon after leaving, we had such a heavy wind-storm that we were compelled to tie up and unable to proceed to Pampur, where we had hoped to pass the night.

We got started very early the following day and went ashore at the Maharaja's palace in Pampur, which is surrounded by very pretty gardens with some beautiful trees. We had two purposes in landing—one was to get some more of the Pampur bread, a large supply of which we had laid in on the way up and liked very much. It is in thin sheets about nine inches in diameter, somewhat resembling a wafer, but tastes like fresh popcorn. Curiously enough it is made nowhere else in Kashmir except in Pampur, and is sent from there all over the Valley. Our other object was to see one of the puttoo mills. This we found to be, as a matter of fact, a sort of hovel, and in the room where the looms were, which was about six by ten, and six and a half feet high, with only two small tightly closed windows and with walls and ceiling as black as ink, there were eight men at work on the looms making this homespun cloth for garments. Sultana bought some twenty-four yards of this material for twenty rupees, which would be six dollars and sixty-six cents, this same material costing in New York about three dollars a yard.

HOLY MEN

At every turn, in the crowded bazaars or in the solitudes of the mountains, these so-called "Holy Men" are seen. They wear little or no clothing, but cover their bodies with oil and then sprinkle themselves with ashes. Their bed is the earth, their shelter the sky and their food whatever they can find or beg.

THE VALE OF KASHMIR

As we were leaving, two very magnificent natives came out in the road and presented us with huge bouquets from the royal gardens. Of course, this meant an acknowledgment in the shape of rupees.

From there to Srinagar we were rowed in the rapid current in a very short time and were fortunate enough to find an even better mooring than we had left when we went up the river.

XXV

GULMARG

"When from power and pomp, and the trophies of war
He flew to that valley, forgetting them all"
—*Lalla Rookh*.

WHILE there are many resorts to which visitors or residents in the Valley go during the hot months of July and August, there is probably none that compares in popularity with Gulmarg. Nor is this due simply to the fact that the Maharaja and the British Resident make it their official summer home, as there are many factors that influence people to choose this as their place of residence for these two months, not the least of which is, in all probability, the exceptionally fine provision made for golf. As the number of people going to Gulmarg the early part of July is very great, it is necessary to make arrangements some time ahead, in order to secure the ekkas, tongas and baggage ponies. Our own provision in this respect had been made some three weeks in advance of the date named, and a large portion of our luggage and effects was sent on the day before, with all of our servants that could be spared. The ekkas were used for some of the larger pieces of luggage and the servants, but most of the effects were strapped on the backs of the luggage ponies, and as they came to the bank just beside the boat it was a very interesting process to witness the cleverness with which the bundles were made up so that they would be equally balanced on either side of the pony.

On the following morning we left with two motors and went straight through from Srinagar to Tangmarg, where we alighted to mount the ponies on which we were to ride when we climbed the mountain path, as it takes about an hour to go from this point to the Valley of Gulmarg. Under ordinary circumstances it is a delightful and glorious ride, but a heavy thunder-storm came up when we were about half

The Royal Post Tonga that carries all the mail in and out of Kashmir, traveling over the pass night and day with remarkable regularity.

The Kashmir sedan. Were it not that the sympathy of the traveler is aroused by the carriers of this peculiar conveyance, this mode of travel would be quite ideal for mountain climbing.

THE VALE OF KASHMIR

way up the mountain and this continued for two or three hours. In consequence we were all thoroughly soaked before we reached the top and naturally in no very favorable mood to appreciate the beauties of the scenery. At last when we arrived at the top of the rim of the mountain that surrounds the so-called Valley of Gulmarg, we realized that this valley is like a basin—a huge emerald basin perched against the mountain wall. From the outer rim of this basin the mountain descends as a sheer precipice to the level of the valley on all sides but one, where it rises in stately slopes to its lofty crest. As this rim and much of the basin itself, as well as portions of the mountain wall, are beautifully wooded with splendid evergreen trees, there are abundant opportunities for bridle-paths and delightful rides. Along the top of this rim are some of the finest summer homes, including those of the British Resident and the Maharaja, while the slopes of the bowl-like valley are dotted in all directions with what are called huts, and some of which are extremely picturesque cottages. Although later on, toward the latter part of July and until after the middle of August, as the number of huts is entirely inadequate, the whole valley looks like a huge encampment because of the large number of white tents that dot it in all directions.

On one of the entrances to the Valley of Gulmarg is the long street of native bazaars that are open only during these few months, as there are no winter residents in Gulmarg and no town, everyone coming from elsewhere for the summer and leaving at the close of the season. People who have gone up in November or March have been struck by the seeming desolation.

On our first rainy advent we became separated from our guide and, as there are no streets in the proper sense of the word and no carriages of any kind (for it would be impossible for one to be brought up the mountain owing to the fact that there are no roads and nothing but narrow bridle-paths), we were not in a mood to feel much interest in anything but find-

THE VALE OF KASHMIR

ing our cottage. This took about four times as long as it ought, because none of us were able to speak the language of the country and we were not fortunate enough to pass any English people or English-speaking natives. However, at last we did reach our compound and found that we had a very comfortable hut, with a fireplace in each room and connecting bath-rooms. We also had a stable in the rear and were surrounded by some of the finest trees on the mountain, while from our veranda, which ran across the whole length of the hut, we had beautiful views of certain portions of the valley and the golf-links only a short distance away. On either side were English neighbors, and across a little brook that skirted the compound was a charming grove which was used by some of the natives as a dairy. At first we were inclined to object to this, but afterward we became quite attached to seeing the cattle go out and come in each day, and enjoyed being able to get all the milk and cream we wanted without the slightest difficulty. Moreover, some of the little calves were allowed to graze in our compound and it gave the place a decidedly bucolic look to see them, with the sheep, geese, chickens, ducks and ponies, all wandering without restraint.

As has been stated elsewhere, there are two roads, the inner and the outer circles, the one being on the inner side of the rim of this bowl—a bowl about two miles long and one-half mile broad—and going, through the trees, all the way around the bowl; and the other on the outer side, which also is in the midst of noble shade trees. The former of course commands a wide variety of charming prospects of the Valley of Gulmarg itself, and the latter of the entire vast stretch of the Valley of Kashmir. These two roads permit a constant diversion of walks and rides and so wide a variety of combinations can one make by going over passes from the outer to the inner road that there ensues a never-failing variety of experiences. As this valley is about eight thousand five hundred feet above the sea it is almost invariably cool, if not cold, and the name Gulmarg, or "Meadow of Roses," seems almost

THE VALE OF KASHMIR

like a misnomer at certain times when you have fires burning in every room throughout the twenty-four hours and even then are unable to keep warm.

One who has visited in Kashmir for a great many years says of Gulmarg: "The climate would be delightful but for the frequent rain, which is at least three times as much as at Srinagar." On the other hand, the scenery and flowers are lovely and the natural advantages of this spot immensely superior to those of any other Himalayan station. The view across the valley in clear weather, which includes the Wular Lake and the snow-capped mural ridges beyond, is certainly magnificent. The Nanga Parbat, although it is ninety miles to the north, lifts its snowy peak nearly twenty-seven thousand feet in the air and can be seen to a beautiful advantage. Indeed, many think it compares very favorably, because of its fascinating spell, with the view of Kinchinjunga from Darjeeling.

XXVI
THE PEOPLE

"Till shame at last, long hidden, burns
Their inmost core, and conscience turns"
—*Lalla Rookh.*

ON this topic it would be easy to write volumes, but we must confine ourselves to a few features of more than general interest, speaking, first of all, perhaps, of the physique. The impression produced is of a people somewhat below the average middle height, and yet for the most part they are remarkably well developed and in some instances almost statuesque. The men, many of whom wear full beards, although it has become fashionable with some of the more up-to-date younger members to affect a mustache, even when they look strong and powerful and are able to do an average amount of manual labor, seem to be wanting in stamina and virility. You have a feeling that there is a lack of toughness and endurance—a suggestion of being washed out and requiring vital substance. The features are ofttimes extremely handsome, almost classic in their regularity, and while the majority are dark and have black eyes and beards, occasionally a blond is to be seen.

The women, who are famed for their beauty, would hardly suggest this renown to the superficial visitor, and yet a longer and fuller acquaintance with them causes one to realize that this reputation for beauty is after all very well deserved, and it would perhaps be impossible to find more perfect features or more beautiful coloring or more exquisite development of form and figure than is occasionally found, especially among the, so to speak, better classes, where there is a seeming refinement and spirituality, that exists more largely in appearance than in reality.

The lower classes, while stronger and more vital, with fuller and better rounded figures, are chiefly suggestive of the animal type of development, although it is animal beauty of

WOMEN SPINNING THREAD IN THE VILLAGE OF SOPOR

No one in Kashmir is in a hurry. What isn't done today will certainly be done tomorrow. But tomorrow is very slow in arriving. The crude primitive methods the people employ certainly do not make for speed. But though progress is slow, all of their handiwork reflects a wonderful skill and a painstaking attention to the minutest details.

THE VALE OF KASHMIR

a very rich and vital kind. This word "vital," however, should be modified by the statement that practically all of the Kashmiri give one the impression of being in a sense physical degenerates. You have a feeling that power and strength and virility should be breathed into them indefinitely in order to have the nature a balanced one. This physical degeneracy is reflected in, or associated with, mental and moral degeneracy, not that all are degenerates, but very few have mental powers of a high order or even an average degree, and, fewer still, moral qualities that would commend themselves as being fine types to one accustomed to Occidental standards. As stated and implied in other chapters, one has a feeling that lying is really the rule, habit and a characteristic, it being more natural to lie than to tell the truth, and to gain a point it is considered the most natural thing to lie in any way or to any degree. This, of course, is rather trying to one when he first comes to the Valley with a different standard, and it is hard when you hear a man or woman tell you a thing, with a perfectly serious, solemn, earnest expression of countenance, although perhaps a vacuous one, and know that in all likelihood there is no truth in anything that is being stated. So common is this habit of lying that they frequently lie when the truth would serve a much better purpose and they seem almost instinctively to lie when it would be much simpler and more helpful to them if they merely stated things as they actually were.

With this mendacity goes, very naturally, a pilfering habit, for it very generally happens that a liar is also a thief. That rule is even more true in the Orient, and especially in Kashmir, than in the West. Indeed, it might almost be accepted as an axiom that very nearly all of them are thieves. So generally is this recognized and accepted even among themselves that practically everything they wish to keep is either put under lock and key or hidden, and the visitor is compelled to keep all his foods locked up, as well as all his provisions. They even steal the kerosene oil. A can of five gallons is found to be

THE VALE OF KASHMIR

going very rapidly, an investigation is made and it is discovered that certain of the servants when they fill the lamps fill some bottles at the same time and carry these bottles to their own portion of the boat and hide them under the boarding of the deck. They even go so far as to steal the fire-wood, which is here bought not by the cord, but by the pound, and is more expensive than most articles in this section of the world. The servants will arrange with one another to take from each purchase a certain percentage for their own use, and it sometimes happens that when a sufficient accumulation of these percentages has been made, the proprietor buys a given quantity of wood that he has already paid for. In other words the stolen wood is sold back to him a second time.

Nor are they any better in the matter of cleanliness, to which reference has been made in other parts of the book. They do bathe, it is true, but their homes are hotbeds of filth and vermin. Frequently they have nothing but a dirt floor that is alive with fleas, and the accumulations of filth about the room are so great and so noxious that there is not only a sickening odor, but a positive danger. It is due to this that they have had such fearful visitations of cholera, smallpox, leprosy, consumption (which is very common), plague (which is often fatal), and enteric diseases, the latter being almost constant. So general are these conditions, that, as stated in connection with the foods, it is unsafe to drink even the pure water—pure from the hydrants, and this is pure until it comes out of the hydrants into the vessel in which it is brought to the house or boat, but that vessel is so contaminated that the water is made unsafe and it is necessary to boil all that one drinks. This is also true of the milk. Nothing could be more dangerous than unboiled milk. So, too, of all uncooked fruits and vegetables—they should be most carefully washed, not with river water or hydrant water, but with boiled water, in order in some measure to rid them from the danger of infection due to these filthy habits and conditions.

SPINNING OUT THE THREAD

The women of Kashmir are famed for their beauty, but your first impression is that they have been overrated. However, after you have seen them at their various tasks and recreations, noted their erect carriage, the undulating grace of their movements, and their flashing eyes, you realize that they have a charm distinctively their own.

TRAVELING BANDS OF MUSICIANS WITH NAUTCH GIRLS

In rythmic sway to the screams and moans of string and wind instruments, these Nautch girls dance in truly Oriental fashion, furnishing entertainment along the roadside, at weddings and festivals. The costumes of the band are exceedingly picturesque, while the shape of their instruments is almost as weird as the sounds they produce.

THE VALE OF KASHMIR

The children are often astonishingly beautiful, the little girls being perfect pictures in their picturesque little clothes, although this beauty has very little staying quality and they become old at an early age.

Their voices are not one of their agreeable features, and it is exceedingly irritating to hear these sharp, shrill, penetrating tones that rasp and tear the nerves of one's ear, especially when they are engaged in violent disputes or a general row is going on.

Over against these somewhat unattractive characteristics it is only fair to put a few statements as to what is being done in the way of character building by Mr. Tyndale-Biscoe, the Neve brothers and others. In view of what has been said, the conditions would seem to be almost hopeless, and yet the amount of good that in a comparatively few years has been done in the way of laying the foundations of character is simply incalculable, and many of these pupils of Mr. Tyndale-Biscoe's school present a striking contrast to what they themselves had been before being subject to this developing influence, and an even more striking contrast to the members of their families and their associates who have not had these advantages.

Here, for instance, the boys are not only taught to be men, but made to be men, with the result that they are strong and vigorous, with an exceptional measure of endurance, and better yet are courageous and brave, even noble, whereas the majority are cowards of the most pitiable kind and show their strength, if they have any, in maltreating their women and the weaker members of the community, as well as their beasts of burden. This tone of vital manliness that has been imparted to the workers under Mr. Tyndale-Biscoe has become a sort of standard, and if you were to lose or have stolen a purse or any article of value and were to go to the police authorities and state the case, you might be assured that everything would be done to regain these, with expressions of sympathy and apologies that such things had taken place, but never receive

THE VALE OF KASHMIR

the articles themselves. Whereas if the services of some of the members of Mr. Tyndale-Biscoe's teaching force could be engaged, the chances are that they would very soon track the rascal and regain the booty. This also applies to their mental development, which while comparatively flabby as a rule, is among these teachers of a remarkably high order. There is a clearness of perception and a strength of mental grasp and readiness of appreciation and comprehension that is very gratifying. They discuss subjects of world-wide interest and view things from a large standpoint. They are also of not only better physical and mental quality, but have fine spiritual ideals. Those that happen to be Hindus are most consistent and wholesome followers of these teachings, or if they are Mohammedans they are truer and more earnest in interpreting the teachings of that cult, and their minds are more open to the essential principles of Christianity in so far as they apply to daily life. This is sometimes very touchingly revealed by unfortunates that have been cared for in the hospitals, or boys who have been taught in the schools. They have gone elsewhere and passed on this gift of rendering service to others, in short the leaven of going about doing good has been imparted to them and they in turn are imparting it to others.

It is entirely fair, therefore, in thinking of the general conditions that seem to prevail, to realize the splendid possibilities that lie before these people in the future.

ANOTHER GLIMPSE OF THE CHENAR BAGH

This beautiful meadow interlaced with canals takes its name from the chenar tree, whose evergreen glory forms one of the most pleasing remembrances of the Vale of Kashmir.

XXVII

AN ARTIST PARADISE

"And, oh! if there be an Elysium on earth,
It is this, it is this"
—*Lalla Rookh.*

THAT this title is fully warranted one can see by simply glancing at the color pictures, some of which are reproductions from beautiful water-colors done by Colonel Hart. From these, too, it will be seen what a wide variety of landscape features, shrubs and trees and flowers and color is to be found in the Valley. These, however, are but distinct expressions of very remarkable natural effects.

The first large body of water seen on entering the Valley—Wular Lake—is also one of its most interesting features, not only because of the striking mountain setting and luxuriant verdure, but more especially perhaps because of the wonderful light, atmospheric and color effects. It is said of Venice that it is almost impossible to paint any color or atmospheric effects that are not to be found at some time or under some circumstances in Venice. This is equally true of the Wular Lake, where the striking natural features are sometimes black and grim, weird and sombre, and at other times fairly glowing with the golden radiance and sheen that so bathes all things that it is almost impossible to realize that this is the same spot you have seen under such strikingly contrasting conditions.

Then, too, one who is sensitive to such beauty is fully conscious that even the most gifted artist is unable to catch the subtlest and most evanescent effects. These are seen and felt, but cannot be either described or reproduced. A sail, therefore, on this lake just after the hour of sunset, when all the landscape is glowing with the various shades of golden light, streaked and blended and mottled with every degree of rosy tinge, and barred and intensified by the deeper shadows of the mountains and islands that are cast athwart the water, is a rare feast, and one perforce sits enraptured, filled with the vain regret that it is impossible to reproduce these remarkable effects so that others who cannot come may be able to see and appreciate. Something of this is perhaps conveyed by the pictures, but it must always be borne in mind that these at best are very feeble suggestions of the indescribable reality. Naturally this lake is a very favorite spot for artists, and many are the efforts that have been made to catch its moods and express them in form and color.

Then as one advances into the Valley after the fields and trees and mountain sides are clad in ever-changing color, one begins to realize how diverse and how continuous is this feast of beauty. The view of vast stretches of poppies under the noble chenar trees, with vistas of the hills and mountains, between which a soft pearly mist rises to refine the somber gloom of the higher mountain wall with its crest of eternal snow, is an experience never to be forgotten, and yet it is one that the lover of the beautiful has day after day.

Another very striking effect is had from Pampur, where, standing some distance back from the river's bank, one looks over a variegated mass of blood-red flowers tinged with golden yellow and deep rich purples peeping from the green of the trees and shrubs, across the blue opalescent water of the river to the maroon-tinted opposite bank, above which in the distance rise the huge trees that are varying masses of yellow or gorgeous revelations of deep red, while still farther in the distance the horizon is bound by the dull violet wall that rises to its snowy crest which extends for nearly eighty miles, with an infinite variety of indentations and configurations.

In still another of the pictures one realizes the fascinating color effects in the mingling of the various shades of yellow and red and green across the purple, or brown tree trunks.

But of all the remarkable effects probably none is more delightful or astonishing than that of the Dhal Lake when the lotus flowers are in bloom. This is so wonderful that nearly everyone in the Valley, no matter how remote he may be

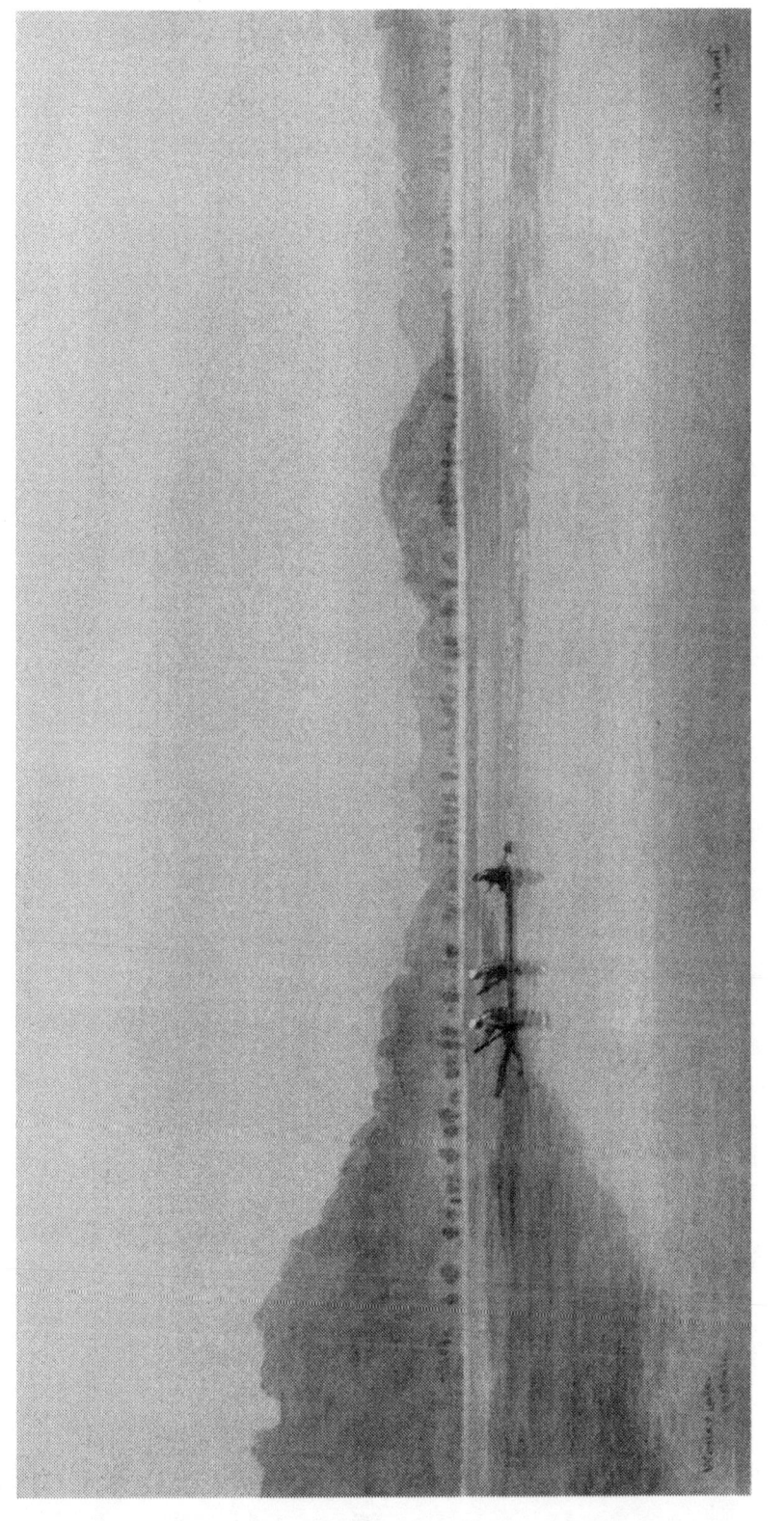

THE VALE OF KASHMIR

from the Lake at the time, tries to visit it and that, too, year after year. Of course it is utterly impossible to convey any idea of how potent is this charm, and yet it not infrequently happens that people who go in boats through the lake at this time are almost intoxicated and overcome by the spell that is cast upon the senses.

This great variety of natural compositions admits of subtle selection, and the artist is able to choose almost anything he wishes from this manifold expression. There are not only the lakes and the canals and the roads and the mountains and the temples, snow and ice, gardens and flowers and the blooms of the trees, and the light effects, but the glorious and refined coloring. The only difficulty lies in the fact that the artist becomes so lost in admiration and in reveling in this feast, and so conscious of his incapacity to reproduce it, that he gives himself up almost exclusively to its enjoyment and makes little, if any, effort to catch and hold it on paper or canvas. It is esteemed, very properly, by many artists to be a sort of Mecca to which one goes to worship the beautiful in nature. The great difficulty is its inaccessibility, not only being so far from Europe, but also from India itself. The time and expense required to make the journey are so great that few are able to undertake it, and yet none have ever been there, at whatever cost, without a feeling of complete satisfaction and more than adequate compensation.

www.ingramcontent.com/pod-product-compliance
Lightning Source LLC
Chambersburg PA
CBHW032022230426
43671CB00005B/176